Studies in Modern and Classical Languages and Literature (III)

Edición a cargo de
RICHARD A. LIMA

EDITORIAL ORIGENES

Colección Tratados de Crítica Literaria

Primera edición: Orígenes, 1990.

© Rollins College.
© Editorial Orígenes.
Plaza de Tuy, 4. ☎ 201 58 00. 28029-Madrid.

Depósito Legal: M - 19055 - 1991
I.S.B.N. 84-7825-038-7

Studies in Modern and Classical Languages and Literature (III)

Edición a cargo de

RICHARD A. LIMA

LITERATURE'S UNRECOGNIZABLE VOICE
OR HEAR ME: IT'S YOU!

I hope it won't seem out of order if I introduce my talk —which aims to communicate something about literature as an experience we have together — by just talking about myself. I'm aiming, eventually, to say something about literature as the place that's common to me and to you — to me, speaking now, and to you, silent — a place, indeed, where, if anyone speaks, it's for another and so that it might be he who talks. Whence my title, the title of my talk to you now — Hear me: It's you. So I hope you won't find it too contradictory if I begin, in a kind of preamble, by talking about the way I myself happen to have been introduced to the study of literature, a little about my evolving experience with literary works and about some of the institutions that have, bit by bit, led to my current thoughts and to my wanting to speak to you.

My favorite teacher, in the first literature courses I took in college, was an extraordinarily gifted practitioner of «Close Reading». As his student I came to believe — with what I now think was a somewhat simplistic faith (simplistic because of my youthful bedazzlement rather than because of any dogmatism on my teacher's part) — that not one word, not a single comma in a given work of literature is there by chance, but that each and every one is absolutely necessary in order for this work to be just what it is — itself, incomparable — and that no other words but its words could ever explain its being so, or approximate its being; but that an ideal interpretation would demonstrate the utter necessity of each word, every phrase, confirming that each is in its inevitable place, not by referring to any determination outside the work, such as the author's preoccupations, his intentions, tastes or commitments, or to the work's historical context (its relation to other, contemporary texts, to social conditions, to economic and political change), but solely by bringing to light the unique character of this specific text itself, unrepresentable in any terms save its very own, irreducible to any logic save the one it comprises in itself. I started out, thus, in my study of literature, as what is called, often for good reasons disparagingly these days, a formalist: weak in literary and intellectual history, relatively insensitive to the complicated mesh of literature with other human endeavors (interactions and struggles), but bent upon appreciating individual works' particular design or structure, in the symmetries and a-symmetries, in the joints and criss-crossing of which I expected lay the secret of their incomparable way of being — themselves, nothing but themselves. And to this day I remain enthralled by literary works like those that stunned me in college — works which, though surely they can be shown to open in multiple ways upon the world outside, and though without a doubt it is very important that they should be so construed and studied (lest they become cult objects, fetishes, and reading turn into idolatry), nevertheless at some level admit of no relations with anything else and stand separate, aloof, offering nothing to be understood except that *there they are*. They are just there, unlike anything else whatsoever. It's still my conviction that their words alone, in their unique configuration, constitute their own sole explanation. And yet, the very works that have impressed me the most, the ones that have made me want to read them over and over, backwards and forwards, studying the particular patterns of each, its characteristic repetitions, its typical oppositions with their axes — learning, in short, the traits that structure each one as if each were a unique language (with its own lexicon and grammar) which I'd like to be able to speak — these very works have taught me to distrust adjectives like *auto-referential, autonymous,* or *self-contained*. For the picture of the literary text as a closed entity, resting complete in itself and itself accounting for all of its parts doesn't seem to me to convey their strangeness. They strike me more and more, the more I study them — locating their joints and hinges, discovering how they operate (according to what law), and how they unfold or draw together in

8

gathers and pleats (determined by what basic contradiction or fundamental paradox) — more and more they strike me as *unbelievable*. I can't, so to speak, get over their just being there, just as they are, and I feel, in my encounters with them, the way the narrator in Melville's novella *Bartleby the Scrivener* feels about Bartleby, his weird employee, the «unaccountable copyist» who unsettles him to an alarming degree by settling in his law office and becoming a veritable fixture there. I feel confronted with literature, *incredulous*. «What, still there?» I'm apt to murmur upon opening a favorite text — just like Bartleby's «thunderstruck» boss upon opening his office in the morning and finding that Bartleby has not departed.

«What are you doing there?» «What in the world justifies your presence?» Bartleby prefers to give no answer. He prefers not to explain or account for himself at all ever. No one who sees him, and solicitously or anxiously of furiously interrogates him, can make anything whatsoever of his being there. But there he is, always there, immovable yet strangely unplaceable (indeed, as often as people try to dislodge him, they try to make him stay put, somewhere or other, wherever it may be that he belongs).

I think, too, of the stone statuette in Nathalie Sarraute's novel *Vous les entendez*. It's not only that no one can figure out what sort of animal it represents, or where it comes from, to what culture it belongs — when, in the history of what people it can have been carved; it's not just that the stone beast bears no resemblance to anything else, and can't be measured or evaluated with respect to any model of satisfactorily described in any available discourse. More disquieting still: it bears no resemblance to itself. And no one can really be sure whether it is good or lousy, beautiful or ugly, exceptional or run-of-the-mill. It is, in fact, *unrecognizable*. Yet, there it is, unmistakable. It's the unrecognizableness — the unrecognizableness and the unbelievableness of literature — that my «formalist» study of it has brought home to me, and not so much the satisfaction — which I suppose I expected — the satisfaction you obtain when the pieces of a marvelous puzzle fit, and you get it (aha!).

A given literary text is unlike anything else, but it's also unlike itself. It differs, as Derrida would say — it simply differs. Which means that it's being just what it is — other, different (incomparable, unique) — excludes its resting in itself.

It's simply a difference. And a difference isn't a thing in itself. It's in between things, a relation between things. The work of literature, then — separate, as I persist in thinking, admitting of no comparison and immeasurable with respect to anything else — isn't an entity enclosed, contained within itself, conforming to itself. Rather, the work is the opening in itself of a difference, an interval, where it's not. And yet the work isn't anything other, or any place other, than this in-between, this interval or rapport. Separate, unique, bearing no relation to anything else. It is nonetheless a relation: it's *sheer* relation. And not, precisely, a relation to itself. All I've said implies that the work doesn't turn back upon itself, referring to itself. It doesn't return to itself and reflect, or reflect upon itself. It doesn't conform to itself. It differs. And it won't, so to speak, hold still. But motionlessly it expends itself simply being just what it is: which is to say other. Other than that. Different.

And this is why I've sometimes thought that the most, if not the only appropriate interpretation of a literary work would be an enactment of this expenditure, a performance of this differing. I've often thought of texts as sheets of music, and once I wrote that all I wanted to do was to play this novel, or that poem: play the notes that are written. I didn't literally suppose that the interpretation a work of literature most urgently calls for is its own repetition word for word, but still I tried to find a way of speaking and writing about my favorite texts that would be equivalent to a singer's interpretation of a song, or an actor's of a role, or to the rhapsodists' interpretation of the poets in ancient times.

I didn't actually suppose that reciting, declaiming — or copying down — a given text was really the performance, or execution I felt more and more called upon to give, but I did wonder why it wasn't. Why did I experience my longing to understand certain texts — my desire, that is, properly to respond to them — as a command, or sometimes something more like a plea coming from the texts themselves — a *Speak me! Say me! Sing me!* — and at the same time know that to repeat, or to recite. But that what is there — what *there is,* unmistakably yet unrecognizably because of literature — is a voice. A voice, which is not anything repeatable or that could be recited. Another way of putting this, and of suggesting in what peculiar sense a piece of literature is always unique — incomparable and impossible to reproduce — would be to say that literature doesn't say anything, save this: You say it! And thus, when I suggest that literature is voice, by voice I mean this utterly implausible thing — this speech that doesn't speak, that says nothing, but that nevertheless says: *It's you. It's you speaking.* So speak?

I believe I began to be somewhat obsessed with that order — *Speak!* — when, a few years ago, I read an account of a torture session, by Marguerite Duras. It was then that I started to think a lot about scenes in which someone tries to make another person talk. I realized that such scenes recur in several of the stories that have had the greatest effect on me: in *Bartleby the Scrivener,* for example. «Will you speak to me today?» Bartleby's anxious employer asks him repeatedly. «Will you answer?» «Why won't you speak?» «Answer me now. Say you'll be a little reasonable and speak to me today», he says. And at length he says, «I know who you are, and I want nothing to say to you».

Or there's the crucial scene in *Billy Budd,* when Billy has to say something. «Speak man!» his captain and judge urges him. «Speak, defend yourself!» Billy must say something, he has got to say the truth. Otherwise it's the gallows for sure. But he can't, he's speechless, overcome by an awful attack of his «vocal defect», his stutter.

Then again, there are the narratives of Louis-René des Forêts, especially the brief stories collected in 1960 in the volume entitled *La Chambre des enfants,* where attempts by certain characters to get others to talk are very numerous. «I come every day», says one of these characters, «to the home of my silent friend, and I give him every day the pleasure of hearing my voice, in hopes that one day he'll give me the pleasure of hearing his». Here are three lines from Hélène Cixous's drama *Chant du corps interdit:* «Tell me who you are for me / Say to me I / Say to me I am here». And finally, in order that they might resonate with the orders — or pleas — that another speak, which I've cited to you, here are two, recurring, sentences from Maurice Blanchot's fragmentary dialogue *L'Attente l'oubli:* «I want to speak to you. Make it so I can speak to you».

I've been pondering, then, on these texts, and one or two others, and not only on the talking and the silence — and the stuttering — in them, but also on the singing; and I've begun to suspect that it is, between literature and me, as it is in these literary works I've mentioned, between the one who wants — another to speak — and the one whose speech is wanting. I've begun, that is, to suspect that I hear coming from literature a voice that wants mine.

I hear a wanting voice; perhaps it's my own.

Ann Smock, Keynote Speaker
University of California, Berkeley

ETHICS IN ACTION AND THE FAILURE OF SPECULATION IN ROBERT MUSIL'S *DIE VERWIRRUNGEN DES ZOGLINGS TORLESS* (1906)

In his first novel *Die Verwirrungen des Zöglings Törless* (1906) [1] Robert Musil presents a thesis on ethics which emerges as philosophical counterpoint to the novel's predominating portrayal of aesthetic amorality among callow youths. Musil centers his thesis upon one moment of ethical decision that occupies little space in the novel but has great value in the strict economy of the text: a single considered action refutes without words the mass of Törless's pondering that are nevertheless necessary for him to gain maturity, viewed as a state of ethical self-understanding.

Törless is about a young man at boarding school in the Austro-Hungarian Empire at the turn of the century. The described space of the novel is in «unwirtlicher Fremde» (16), —remote, lifeless and monochrome: «Machten es diese traurigen Farben, machte es das bleiche, kraftlose,, durch den Dunst ermüdete Licht der Nachmittagssonne: Gegenstände und Menschen hatten etwas Gleichgültiges, Lebloses, Mechanisches an sich, als seien sie aus der Szene eines Puppentheaters genommen» (15). Musil reduces the physical setting of the novel to a scenario of endless monotony and predictable uniformity, which the school regimen will only extend; the only sign of life in the geometric composition of the opening scene is «eine heitere Gesellschaft junger Leute» surrounding Törless and his parents. In the manner of a classical portraitist Musil eliminates background in order to make his reader

---

[1] Robert Musil, *Prosa, Dramen Späte Briefe,* ed. Adolf Frise (Rowohlt: Hamburg, 1957).

concentrate on the psychological qualities of his subject Törless, and indirectly, on his relations to his companions and his parents.

The departure of the parents constitutes the first half of the frame construction of the novel; their reappearance completes the frame and ends the novel. Though scarcely present in the narrative, his parents embody for Törless a world of secure values, whose loss gives rise to his confusions. His parents leave him: «da sich das Tor des Institutes unwiderruflich hinter ihm geschlossen hatte, litt der kleine Törless an fürchterlichem, leidenschaftlichem Heimweh... (16). As his name allegorically signals, Törless is cut off from the outside world of his parents; his isolation at the institute becomes a type of psychological laboratory where all external conditions are held constant in order for Törless (and Musil) to investigate the uneasiness within him: «Er hielt es für Heimweh, für Verlangen nach seinen Eltern. In Wirklichkeit war es aber etwas viel Unbestimmteres...» (17). Beneath the surface of daily events, the principal drama of Musil's small novel of ideas consists in Törless's pursuit of a definitive resolution to the undefined dilemma that causes his suffering. Like Kafka's K. before the castle, young Törless seeks an answer to his questions; he departs onto a cerebral plane in an interrogatory quest for a more orderly world, but the more he seeks, the more he gets lost and finds himself, increasingly desperate, back again where he began.

Törless's thoughts revolve continually around the same point that he can never reach through speculation, where rational thought and irrational feeling coincide. Young Törless cannot accept the inherent contradiction between the two and seeks their reconciliation. In the course of his inner quest he ranges from passionate defiance of adversity to abject indifference, but each assault on the impossible results in an added psychological nuance to the same unchanging conflict. In his thoughts he struggles to accommodate his awakening sexuality, which in turn drives his thoughts toward increasingly abstract indirections.

In effect, his suffering is both cause and symptom of his dilemma, both path and goal to his quest, since what he seeks is unattainable. Throughout the novel each troubling circumstance, each conflict with his companions or with himself is

14

actually only «Gelegenheitsursache, dieses egoistische Leiden in sich zu erzuegen, ...» (17). Therefore, although the escalation of events and increasing refinement of his thinking give the appearance of progressive or organic character development, of «einer bestimmten seelischen Entwicklung» (18), the essential pattern of his thoughts remains the same, continually reversing or qualifying itself with no actual forward progress. *Törless* is not a *Bildungsroman* and does not depict the protagonist's gradual accession to the wisdom of maturity: rather, *Törless* depicts the gradual circumstantial complication of Törless's vain reflections, which results finally in the cumulative, spontaneous overthrow of those circumstances and of those reflections at the end of the novel.

The circumstances that provoke Törless's continuing «confusions» escalate toward his acquiescence in the mistreatment of the androgynous Basini [2]. Basini's mistreatment, however, never reaches its planned climax. Törless intervenes. He recalls a letter from his parents in response to his description of his «sonderbaren Seelenzuständen...» (135). At the time he considered their letter «wieder eine recht hausbackene Antwort, voll rechtschaffener, langweiliger Ethik...» (135), but now he views the letter in a different light: «Heute aber langte er ganz anders nach dieser Stelle, als sie ihm wieder einfiel» (135). The deeply ingrained values of his parents, from which he had been cut off, now appear to Törless as a solution to his dilemma at a moment of apparently irresoluble conflict; his parents' dull ethics occur in Musil's plot as a type of psychologically conceived *deus ex machina*. With his parents' letter in mind Törless makes the ethical decision to call an end to the sadistic experiments of his companions Beineberg and Reiting and to save their victim Basini from further torment:

> Die Entscheidung war in diesem Augenblick gefallen. Ein Gedanke war in ihm aufgeblitzt, und er hatte ihn bedenkenlos ergriffen, gleichsam unter dem Patronale seiner Eltern (135).

---

[2] Cf. Todd Kontje «Organized Violence/Violating Order: Robert Musil's *Die Verwirrungen des Zöglings Törless*», *Seminar*, 24.3 (September, 1988). A lucid examination of Törless's fascination with violence and its implications.

The confusions of Törless come to a sudden end when he accepts the personal responsibility to make a choice and act upon it for the sake of another according to his own *objective* assessment of the situation. With the single thought «bedenkenlos ergriffen» that he must act, Törless steps out of the cycle of futile speculations that had preoccupied him.

Törless tips off Basini to turn himself over to school authorities for his own protection. In the ensuing uproar, Törless runs away; by leaving school precincts he literally breaks free from his tortured isolation and achieves objective distance from his own thoughtful self-involvement. He has recognized the futility and the vanity of his «confusions» and abandoned his intellectual quest. Soon brought back to the school, he delivers a type of peroration before the school board, in which he renounces his errant search for a reconciliation of irreconcilable terms: «Ich weiss, dass ich mich doch geirrt habe. Ich fürchte nichts mehr. Ich weiss: die Dinge sind die Dinge und werden es wohl immer bleiben; und ich werde sie wohl immer bald so, bald so ansehen. Bald mit den Augen des Verstandes, bald mit den anderen... Und ich werde nicht mehr versuchen, dies miteinander zu vergleichen...» (143-144). Within himself Törless has discovered the ethical strength to accept the limitations of intellect in order to act responsibly in the real world; he rejects the solipsism of youth for the understanding of maturity.

Törless summons his parents to remove him from the boarding school. The one-sentence paragraph set apart in the text marks the second half of the frame construction (144) as well as Törless's return to the world of stable values that he had left in the opening scene and whose opposite he found in the amorality of his school companions. Yet he does not return unchanged, nor does he adopt unconsidered the complacent security of his parents' values. His deliberate decision to act according to a personal ethics, though drawing upon his parents' values, does not deny or denigrate the irrational side of experience, «den dunklen Boden des Innersten» (143) that he discovered through his suffering. Earlier plagued by the ambiguity of all knowledge, Törless now leaves school with the confidence of a skeptic in the doubleness of all things, as reflected in the last line of the book: «Und er prüfte den leise

parfümierten Geruch, der aus der Taille seiner Mutter auf-
stieg». In a moment comparable in its poignancy to the last
scene of Kafka's «Die Verwandlung», Törless now recognizes
beneath his mother's bourgeois appearance the concealed, per-
fumed scent of animal sexuality. Each image or idea contains
for Törless its opposite, the inverse of its apparent values.

The cynicism of the final scene comes as no surprise. Musil
has prepared the reader by allowing a satiric view into Törless's future, interpolated before the last fifth of the book
(118-119). Törless appears as a young man, a dandy, an aesthete whose life is «einseitig schöngeistig zugeschärft, ...» (118)
concentrated solely upon «das Wachstum der Seele...» (118).
At that point Törless feels no compunction about his youthful
excesses. Rather, he views the world with a profound moral
indifference calculated to discover in whatever experience an
added subtlety to his inner life. In retrospect the aesthete
Törless derives from the episode with Basini at the boarding
school «jene kleine Menge Giftes, die nötig ist, um der Seele
die allzu sichere und beruhigte Gesundheit zu nehmen und ihr
dafür eine feinere, zugeschärfte, verstehende zu geben» (119).
The final scene of the book shows in Törless the germ of this
cynicism before it reaches decisive articulation by the young
adult.

The interpolated flash forward, or prolepsis, accomplishes
two things: first, the account of the dandy-cynic Törless prevents the reader from seeking a steady «development» in his
character as the book ends. Törless has jumped from having
«keinen Charakter» (21) in his susceptibility to outside influen-
ces to having the overdetermined character of a set type, from
one extreme to the other, both of which deny the wholeness
or depth of ethical character we look for as the proper result
of «Bildung». Second, the flash forward interrupts our reading
of the novel as continuous narrative and reminds the reader
of its formal construction in spatial terms; the flash forward
is mounted in the narrative out of any narrative sequence and
thereby calls attention to the highly artificial use of the frame
construction to contain Törless's errant confusions. With these
two purposes in mind, we see that the flash forward serves
to frame, within the larger frame construction of the novel,
Törless's isolated *moment* of decision, where he achieves real

depth of ethical character, as opposed to the apparent depth of his vain reflections. Nevertheless, that moment remains isolated outside of any development or «Bildung» of character; instead, it marks the reversal of Törless's intellectual disposition from the uncertainty of his quest to the disillusioned certainty of cynicism. Yet in Törless's moment of decision Musil posits a refutation of both unquestioned bourgeois morality (parents and school masters) and of voyeuristic, intellectual amorality, or moral relativism (Törless before and after), and he suggest their reconciliation in the consciousness of one's own personal ethics, not prescribed in advance, but dependent on the circumstances of a distinct situation and realized at the moment of decision *to act* within that situation [3].

Ethical action connects reflective thought to life and human activity; ethical action unites, so to speak, the surface and depth of human experience. Once we have Törless's discrete moment of ethical action as a framed point of reference at the end of the novel, and once we have seen the overall frame construction of the novel, we can understand in retrospect the spatial form of the novel in its parts. Although Törless's reflections are the apparent topic of the novel, Musil's thesis on ethical action emerges as his primary concern. Törless's ethical decision acts as counterweight to the ideational relativism of schoolboy Törless and to the later cynical detachment of Törless the dandy.

Measured against the real depth of his ethical action, Törless's reflections are vain and superficial, though appearances are the opposite; his thoughts seem profound because complex, but they are without ethical value and do not lead *necessarily* to his ethical decision at the end of the novel, which is spontaneous. Without causal relations to his later ethical decision, his confusions reflect, each in its own right, the static construction of the novel as a whole. His reflections

---

[3] Heribert Brosthaus, *Der Entwicklungsroman einer Idee. Untersuchungen zu Gehalt, Struktur und Stil in Robert Musils 'Die Verwirrungen des Zöglings Törless'* (diss. Würzburg, 1969). An important study, though difficult to locate. He comments perceptively: «Die dem Werk immanente Ethik ist... eine schöpferische Einstellung des Individuellen auf das Jeweilige; sie sucht keine Beruhigung im Allgemeinverbindlichen...» (103).

relate to one another, apart from the sudden decision that resolves the plot of the novel, as variations on the fundamental epistemological problem of the ambiguity of all knowledge once freed of ethical responsibility or moral values [4].

Neil H. Donahue
Hofstra University

[4] See David S Luft, *Robert Musil and the Crisis of European Culture 1880-1942* (University of California Press; Berkeley, 1980). Luft describes the sense of intellectual drift that afflicted the «Generation of 1905». Of Musil, in particular, he gives the following perspective on the conflict that shaped Musil's career: «the young scientist adopted the style of the aesthete while seeking to transform his new perceptions in the direction of an ethical art» (23).

JEAN BAUDRILLARD'S AMERICA: IN THE BELLY
OF THE SIMULACRUM

If the chief topic of Jean Baudrillard's new book *America*, after all, is its place in the (European) mental topography, rather than the lay of a land where things really happen and people in fact live and die, then Baudrillard is the perfect man to explore this topic, having in effect had unreal (or «hyperreal») America as one of his themes for a long time.

Baudrillard's is the theory of the simulacrum, and of the hyperrealism that now suffuses it. It is Baudrillard's argument that as the system of consumer society perfects itself, it becomes increasingly adept at producing images of sovereign indifference to either reality or desire, a «divine irreference» in his term: «The real is produced from miniaturized units, from matrices, memory banks and command models — and with these it can be reproduced an indefinite number of times. It no longer has to be rational, since it is no longer measured against some ideal or negative instance. It is nothing more than operational. In fact, since it is no longer enveloped by an imaginary it is no longer real at all. It is a hyperreal: the product of an irradiating synthesis of combinatory models in a hyperspace without atmosphere» [1]. If the simulacrum may properly be said to have a home at all, it would be America; and within America, of course, that media Mecca which provides Baudrillard so many instances of the simulacrum, California [2]. Indeed, true to its own (un)spiritual home, Baudrillard's own travel diary spends a brief time in New York, shi-

---

[1] *Selected Writings*, ed. Mark Poster (Stanford: Stanford University Press, 1988); p. 167.

[2] Baudrillard's interest in California's products is longstanding. Cf. his *Simulacres et simulation* (Paris: Editions Galilée, 1981). esp. pp. 69-91, which treat *Holocaust, The China Syndrome* and

vers perfunctorily in and out of Minneapolis-St. Paul, and tarries most of the time in the land of surf and sun. «Tarries» may not be the word for what he does in this land devoted above all to life in the fast lane: a speedy freeway existence that calls forth some of Baudrillard's purplest eloquence.

It is no accident that Baudrillard's favorite terms for this phenomenon of simulation — «scenario» and «model» — each attach strongly to California sites such as Hollywood and the Silicon Valley. To the extent that Baudrillard would admit of any predecessor for this «take» on postmodernity, it would be Marshall McLuhan, whose incantation «The medium is the message» signals for Baudrillard «not only the end of the message, but also the end of the medium — that is, medium as the mediating element between one reality and another, between one state of reality and another» [3].

It is in the spirit of this view of postmodernity as that state where appearances are the only reality that Baudrillard makes his pilgrimage to America, that land where the «*dessert of the real itself*» meets «the sacred horizon of appearances» to produce the effect Baudrillard sees as most emblematic of this society: the mirage [4].

One of the mirages Baudrillard spies everywhere (although one suspects most frequently in California) is the American smile: «they certainly do smile at you here, though neither from courtesy, nor from an effort to charm. This smile signifies only the need to smile. It is a bit like the Cheshire Cat's grin: it continues to float on faces long after all emotion has disappeared... No ulterior motive lurks behind it, but it keeps you at a distance. It is part of the general cryogenization of emotions. It is, indeed, the smile the dead man will wear in his funeral home, as he clings to a hope of maintaining contact even in the next world. The smile of immunity, the smile of advertising: "This country is good. I am good. We are the best." It is also Reagan's smile — the culmination of the self-satisfaction of the entire American nation — which is on the

_____

Apocalypse Now as hyperreal renderings of a now largely imaginary —Baudrillard would say «fictional»— history.

[3] *Simulacres*, p. 149: «pas seulement la fin du message, mais aussi la fin du medium c'est-à-dire d'instance médiatrice d'une réalité à une autre, d'un état du réel à un autre». Trans. mine.

[4] *Selected Writings;* p. 166; p. 149.

way to becoming the sole principle of government. An auto-prophetic smile, like all smiles in advertising. Smile and others will smile back. Smile to show how transparent, how candid you are. Smile if you have nothing to say. Most of all, do not hide the fact you have nothing to say nor your total indifference to others... Americans may have no identity, but they do have wonderful teeth» [5].

This smile is indeed like that of the Cheshire Cat: the American who wears it is subjected to a process of deconstruction, of etherealization into theory. Whether she or he had in truth had any identity before being transformed into Baudrillard's exhibit A corpse, there would be nothing left to identify her or him (except perhaps those teeth). Yet there is a phantasmagoric logic to the passage. Granted, something about the fatuous optimism implied by this 1986 smile already seems dated: three years later, Reagan's successor is telling everyone to read his lips — and, like those of growing numbers of his countrymen, the lips snarl more than smile. Still, Baudrillard's larger point may be preserved: Bush's lips are to be read as referring less to taxes or some other affair of state than to Bush's need to convey toughness (that is, like the smile, the snarl refers ultimately to itself).

Reading the Baudrillard snarl, and the occasional smile, is not quite so simple. The offhandedness of some of Baudrillard's traveloguish remarks in this text may throw readers off; for he sees America much as other European colonizers have done; as virgin territory, open to intellectual exploration. It is for him a vast space on which to deploy his grand theory of the hyperreal and the simulacrum, those larger-than-life projections not of the imagination but of those systems of mass manipulation — advertising, the media and politics — who make values and keep them circulating: «It may be that the truth of America can only be seen by a European, since he alone will discover here the perfect simulacrum — that of the immanence and material transcription of all values. The Americans, for their part, have no sense of simulation. They are themselves simulation in its most developed state, but they have no language in which to describe it, since they themselves

_____

[5] *America*, tr. Chris Turner (London: Verso Books, 1988), pp. 33-34. All subsequent references are in the body of the text.

23

are the model» (pp. 28-29). It is for this reason, then, that Baudrillard has learned to stop worrying and love the «giant hologram» that is America: he feels it is such a perfect repository of the world his theory would describe (p. 29). This artificial paradise with its shimmering commodities, its «lifestyles» and its toothpaste grins is all Baudrillard sees because it makes his theory seem truer.

No doubt Baudrillard does play the passionate pilgrim, the wayfarer open to the confrontation with the new. Finally, however, despite his claims that «there is no truth of America» (p. 27), and that «*the mystery of American reality* exceeds our fictions and interpretations» (p. 98) — for all that, Baudrillard's interest in the variety of the United States always has a unitary theoretical agenda. The multiplicity of goods, fashions and enthusiasms reduce to the elements of a ballet of consumer society's codes and images, in the same way as the immensely various natural environment also gets reduced to one vast wasteland, the desert.

By thinning out those features of the American landscape not reducible to simulacra, Baudrillard renders it a better staging area for his theory of postmodernity: «We [Europeans] criticize Americans for not being able either to analyse or conceptualize. But this is a wrong-headed critique. It is we [Europeans] who imagine that... nothing exists which has not been conceptualized. Not only do they [Americans] care little for such a view, but their perspective is the very opposite: it is not conceptualizing reality, but realizing concepts and materializing ideas that interests them» (p. 84). This sounds at first like the usual comment on the practicality of Americans. It becomes another way of seeing the US as the land caught up in media-fed fictions, since it is chiefly the communications industry that realizes these concepts and ideas: «For the materiality of things is, of course, their cinematography» (p. 85). It appears, not surprisingly, that the «ideas» Americans «materialize» best bear a strong resemblance to those of Jean Baudrillard.

As with any experiment, Baudrillard's laboratory requires that the subjects be unknowing: a blind study is always best. Luckily, America is to modernity exactly the sort of naive culture that primitive societies were for anthropologists examining ancient life: «It is in this belief in facts, in the total

24

credibility of what is done or seen, in this pragmatic evidence of things... that the Americans are a true utopian society... You have to be utopian to think that in a human order, of whatever nature, things can be as plain and straightforward as that» (p. 85). Such a view leaves little room for, among other things, the paranoid political style that has always been a recurrent mode of our collective life. But it does make Americans conveniently bland and trusting receptacles of consumer society's images, thus rendering Baudrillard's theories a great service [6].

It is fair to say that Baudrillard is duly grateful for this service. He goes to the sacred places of postmodern pilgrimages — he follows Frederic Jameson's footsteps to the Bonaventure Hotel in Los Angeles, for example — and, like Ernest Hemingway's Paris, the US always gives him what he asks of it. Yet the tone often betrays the drama of grand narratives forsaken. Baudrillard, theorist of the end of history, is unable to give the Enlightenment story its proper burial: «You are born modern, you do not become so. And we [Europeans] have never become so» (p. 73). Much as he breezily denies to Americans the capacity to mourn the pathos of the lost referent, he still hesitates to deny this to himself. The belief that American psychology exists in a different temporal relation to Utopia than does Europe (roughly speaking, after rather than before) helps to explain the seeming contradiction that Americans on the hand are always put into opposition to Europeans, and on the other are presented as the dialectical truth of Europe, its destiny. The temporal *trompe l'oeil* of achieved Utopia is one way Baudrillard accounts for this dual status. The same (post)modernity characterized Europe and the US both. But Europe has the baggage of the past; and France's version of that baggage is «the bourgeois model of 1789 — and the interminable decadence of that model» (p. 73). That baggage interferes with France's embrace of the postmodern

---

[6] Other theorists of contemporary media have not subscribed to Baudrillard's view of the literal-mindedness of postmodern American forms. Mark Crispin Miller, for instance, has gone so far as to argue that irony itself is a principal weapon used by TV sitcoms in order to enforce a certain conformity upon its audience. See his article entitled «Big Brother Is You, Watching» (*The Georgia Review*, XXXVIII, 4, Winter 1984; pp. 695-719).

condition, whereas America, by its very primitivism, is free to embrace that same condition.

Stuck in the rut of the «nineteenth-century bourgeois dream» as he is, Baudrillard looks enviously upon the malleability of the American persona in this land of Gatsby: «America ducks the question of origins; ... it has no past and no founding myth. ... It has no ancestral territory. ... America has no identity problem. In the future, power will belong to those people with no origins and no authenticity who know how to exploit that situation to the full» (p. 76). Cynicsm and perpetual innocence are here as one, as the American personality instinctively adopts roles according to need; and there is no consequent guilt over betraying one's origins, because those origins are modernity itself. The fuller portrait of that Cheshire-Cat grin now comes into focus. The very lack of culture's accumulated time — the desert of symbolic reference — makes it all the easier for Americans to fashion themselves according to changing exigencies, because no inner prohibitions outstrip expediency.

Of course, one may accuse Baudrillard's theory of being just as driven by expediency. In any case, Baudrillard does not on his own account concern himself much with the «reality» of what he treats. Sylvere Lotringer, in mentioning to him the metaphor of «woman-object» used in Baudrillard's book *On Seduction*, prompts this revealing response: «I consider woman the absence of desire. It is of little import whether or not that corresponds to real women. It is my conception of "femininity"» [7]. Similarly, no doubt, Jean Baudrillard's America, he would surely claim, is not necessarily any close relation to the real thing: just a giddy simulacrum, or perhaps a hysterical symptom of Baudrillard's own theory.

At one point, he remarks of American power that it «has entered a phase of hysteresis. Hysteresis: the process whereby something continues to develop by inertia, whereby an effect persists even when its cause has disappeared» (p. 115). America for Baudrillard resembles Alfred Jarry's cyclist, «who has died of exhaustion... but who carries on pedalling and propelling the Great Machine» (p. 115). One begins here to see the virtue in the sheer speed Baudrillard exalts. The world seen

[7] «Forget Baudrillard», in *Forget Foucault* (New York: Columbia Semiotext(e), 1987); p. 95.

through the rearview mirror moves by so quickly anything can be imputed to it; and just as quickly, Baudrillard's theorization of what he sees can take off, can go into overdrive. It becomes, to the practitioner of hysteresis, a positive advantage not to know that the Mystic Transportation truck he sees in New York probably refers to Mystic, Connecticut, just up I-95. Better that it be denuded of context, so as to be the vehicle for the author's own kind of mystic transport (pp. 21-22).

Useless to counterpose some real America to compete with his simulacrum (who can purport to have found such a place and who would undertake to describe it?). Best, however, to bear in mind at all times the dual agenda of the book; to dramatize certain very pregnant theories of its author, and to render some impressions of a briefly visited foreign country. Those impressions are rather quickly subsumed into the theoretical machine of Baudrillard; and his journey eventually «moves through space of its own volition ... exactly as the jet engine is no longer an energy of space-penetration, but propels itself by creating a vacuum in front of it that sucks it forward, instead of supporting itself, as in the traditional model, upon the air's resistance» (pp. 10-11). Baudrillard's prose likewise forsakes the resistance of its subject rather quickly.

Whether or not the pilot of this engine of theory approaches the condition of Jarry's cyclist, being along for the ride is often exhiliarating in the way that driving in the desert can be. It is in this connection fitting that Baudrillard ends his reflections in the desert as well, where the real meets the sacred horizon of appearances, and the America of his imagination shimmers mirage-like, beckoning and ever receding before the traveler's gaze.

Mark Conroy
Ohio State University

RESTORING THE MILLENNIUM TO
SEVENTEENTH-CENTURY UTOPIAS

These ten years since the publication of the magisterial *Utopian Thought in the Western World* by Frank and Fritzie Manuel [1] do not suffice wholly to restore confidence that it is possible to present anything on the topic that can be both original and true.

Even the German scene, generally just past the right hand field of vision of most North Atlantic scholars not specifically German or Germanist, receives fair treatment at their hands (pages 289-331), «fair» insofar as German developments contributed directly to the aspects of their study described by the «Western» in their title. This includes, on the hictoric side Valentin Andreae and the foundation documents of Rosicrucianism, Comenius and the Pansophie, Samuel Hartlib and the forerunners of the Royal Society of London, and on the more modern side, «Marx and Counter-Marx» (695-756).

Utopia was the focus of their study, and in consequence, those adjacent ides that project other kinds of perfect universes quite properly assumed secondary importance, as for example, the pastoral, science fiction, and more pointedly for the present purpose, millennialism. They did not ignore these important matters, but they subordinated them to their greater theme. The following argument seeks to suggest that one of these adjacent ideas, millennialism, is less a variant of «Utopia» than the other way around, and that, millennialism pervasively informs Utopia, certainly the Utopia of seventeenth-century middle-Europe and probably all others as well.

The term «utopian» in modern parlance has a connotative

---

[1] (Cambridge, MA: Belknap, 1979).

value not far from that of «quixotic». It expresses an idealistic and well-motivated but not altogether rational, or, if rational, not altogether practical or realistic approach to the practical and real problems of present time and place.

The factors of Time and Place critically distinguish «Utopia» and the «utopian» internally and from similar but not identical expressions and do so for several good reasons. These include 1) the self-definition contained in the terms by etymology, 2) the overlap between Utopia and the «Golden Age», and 3) the instability of particulars in utopian programs, that is, the particulars of one era's utopia may be another era's horror or, conversely, another era's social policy, and yet another era's long desired and finally achieved day-to-day reality.

The factor of Place determines Utopia insofar as Utopia is conceived, despite the Morean pun, as occupying a specific geography, the specificity of which often occupies huge stretches of the literary presentations. These descriptions may lay out a symbolic or, on the other hand, a socially pragmatic program, or both. For the purposes of differentiation, it is the spatial setting of Utopia which distinguishes it from other critiques of the here and now, the principal dimension of which is temporal. That is to say, what Utopia is to Place, the Golden Age, for example, is to Time, with the added complexity that the Golden Age resides at either the beginning or the end of time, or both. The Golden Age and Utopia commonly represent a radical alternativity to the state of affairs prevailing in the here and now. They stand for radically «other» time and radically «other» place, the not here and the not now [2].

Verbal representations of the Golden Age, with precious few exceptions, suffer gravely under the «otherness» imperative. One may argue whether the Garden of Eden is chiefly spatial or temporal. The biblical account locates the Garden quite specifically and suggests that it continues to exist, though impossible ever again to enter, after the primordial pair have been banished. Coming as it does at the beginning of the bi-

---

[2] Sven-Aage Jorgensen, «Utopistisches Potential in der Bibel: Mythos, Eschatologie und Säkularisation», *Utopieforschung*, 3 vols. (Frankfurt: Suhrkamp, 1985), 1, 375-401, here pp. 379-383, for a distinction between «Raumutopie» and «Zeitutopie».

blical narrative and as a continuation of the creation story, the Garden serves as much a chronological function, which has come to dominate its subsequent conceptualization. Its hopeless inaccessibility and its human habitation only at the beginning of things have finally robbed its spatial dimension of relevance. Let Eden therefore stand for one expression of the «Golden Age».

What characterizes the primordial human condition in the Hebrew scriptures is the mastery of man over nature in Genesis 1; the same motif is carried over into the creation of Adam in Genesis 2, where «life» in the Garden is specified as innocent and seems occupied mostly by the naming of the animals. Only in Genesis 3, when pain, labor, the obstinacy of the earth, and death are inflicted on the primordial pair is it clear what they have lost. The Garden is not, in fact, fully defined until the expulsion, that is, in terms of a negation of what is generally known about the human condition [3].

The fundamentally negative representation of the first times is somewhat more obviously portrayed in Hesiod's description of the Time of the Golden Race, «when Cronos was king of heaven ... like gods they lived with hearts free from sorrow and remote from toil and grief ... nor was miserable age their lot, but always unwearied in feet and hands they made merry in feasting, beyond the reach of all evils ... the fertile earth spontaneously bore them abundant fruits ... and they lived in ease and peace upon their lands with many good things, rich in flocks and beloved of the blessed gods». The negations of the first part of the description declare frankly what the positive succeeding descriptions barely conceal: that life among the Golden Generation was the opposite of ordinary life in the world.

The elements of the descriptions of the primordial condition do not chiefly refer to one another but rather to their opposites in another composition altogether in which the relationships are experiential and autonomous, human life in the world as it is.

In both these descriptions and many others from around the world, the easy, want-free, struggle-free primordial time shares this quality of a photonegative and , like a photonega-

---

[3] Ibid., p. 375.

tive, when processed, reveals something about what the myth-makers really objected to in their lives.

Golden Ages from around the world share another quality, and that is the risk of sliding into Cockaigne, Schlaraffenland, and right down the Big Rock Candy Mountain. One attribute alone wards off the high risk of the ridiculous, and that is the presence of the deity or a surrogate, without whom all this licence, ease, and abundance becomes absurd.

For a Golden Age to be serious, it must have a close relationship with some divine or transcendent force. It lacks autonomy, that is, it acts as a negative allegory of the present. Furthermore, a primordial Golden Age, by definition, must come to an end. As the dependencies and limitations accumulate around the concept of the Golden Age, its true nature begins to reveal itself. It is not an independent model of a perfect condition but only one small part of a process, which includes 1) its inevitable decay or catastrophic conclusion, 2) the present woefully inadequate world, which is not just in a bad condition but is daily getting worse, 3) an imminent catastrophe resulting from the degeneration of the present condition (and corresponding to the event or process which ended the primordial Golden Age in the first place), and 4) a restoration of the Golden Age, however, without the implicit defect that led to its original demise [4].

In this context, the Golden Age reveals itself a fragmentary manifestation of the apocalyptic worldview, the distribution of which around the world frankly dwarfs the literary Utopia and all its permutations. The same may be said of the concrete social manifestations of these ideas: in the case of apocalypticism, millennial outbreaks, which across history greatly outnumber utopian experiments, although both incline to end «by bringing great suffering upon their members» [5].

The seventeenth-century West, which is here a net loosely cast to snag Russia and the Jewish Middle East as well as the rest of Europe and America, witnessed a great variety of millennial outbreaks, the most dramatic of which are probably

---

[4] Comp. Bernard McGinn, *Visions of the End: Apocalyptic Traditions in the Middle Ages* (New York: Columbia University Press. 1979), pp. 10-11.
[5] Manuel, p. 807.

the appearance of the Fifth Monarchy Men in England [6], of the schismatic Old Believers in Russia [7], and of the «mystical messiah», Sabbatai Sevi, among the Jews of the Old and New Worlds [8]. The full impact of these movements was felt in the second half of the century, approaching and succeeding the millennial (plus Triumphant Beast) year of 1666.

Their simultaneous appearance is largely or entirely coincidental, that is to say, none can be causally related to the other, although news travelled fast along the trade routes, and what happened in Smyrna would soon be published in Amsterdam, touch colonists in the West Indies, and provide Increase Mather with materials for sermons in Boston [9].

The apparent absence of a similarly dramatic outbreak among Christians of Middle Europe should not be disturbing, since millennialism was pervasively available to them in their literature (e. g, Moscherosch, Grimmelshausen) and among countless sects, of whom the Moravians are perhaps the best known. Furthermore, recent historical digging has unearthed a large and important eschatological literature written by the very hands of those who were shaping Lutheran orthodoxy and, at least superficially, condemning the sectarians who sought to establish God's kingdom on earth. These hands include Luther's own, who despaired of history and, like many others, tried, late in life, to calculate the years remaining before the Second Coming [10].

Even without this context, Andreae's early and repeated disavowal of the Rosicrucian fiction and of the millennial in the *Christianopolis* would indicate that there was a problem, that there were those who would read his constructs as plans

  6 P. G. Rogers, *The Fifth Monarchy Men* (London: Oxford University Press, 1966); B. S. Capp, *The Fifth Monarchy Men* (London: Faber & Faber, 1972).

  7 Robert O. Crummey, *The Old Believers and the World of Antichrist* (Madison: University of Wisconsin Press, 1970).

  8 Gershom Scholem, *Sabbattai Sevi: The Mystical Messiah* (Princeton: Princeton University Press, 1973).

  9 Ibid., pp. 102, 549.

  10 Robin Bruce Barnes, *Prophecy and Gnosis: Apocalypticism in the Wake of the Lutheran Reformation* (Stanford: Stanford University Press, 1988), pp. 46-53. Arguing for a persistently apocalyptic Luther (not just «old» Luther): Heiko Obermann, «Teufelsdreck: Eschatology and Scatology in the "Old" Luther», *Sixteenth Century Journal*, 19, 3 (Fall 1988), 435-450.

for imminent realization and not, as the old Andreae would have it, a *paradigma* irrelevant to life in this vale of tears (Manuel, p. 308).

A clear instance of this problem is Jan Comenius, who wrote his first Utopia (in Czech), lifted from Andreae's was trying to shake off responsibility for the Rosicrucian fiction (1623). Comenius's *Labyrinth of the World* qualifies as a negative Utopia. The explicit criticism of the world he visits guided by Searchall Ubiquitous, servant of Queen Vanity, and in the company of Delusion, refers to the world as it is, and chiefly by magnification, holds it up to criticism [11]. The surface of the work shows a radically repudiating posture over against the misery, dishonesty, and violence of the world. The evidence for millennialism is at best indirect: a certain conformity which the «signs» predicting the imminent end of all this evil and a disturbing epiphany of Seven Wise Men, awakened by God to restore the true alchemy [12]. The degree to which the world is rejected allows only two exits: one vertical, into mysticism; one horizontal, into a time when these conditions no longer prevail.

That Comenius awaited the moment of the second exit is indisputable. He pursued every chiliastic prophet he could find on his wanderings (Peuckert, p. 180). Early in his life, he came under the influence of Mikulas Drabik, a visionary and «prophet» whom he never repudiated, even when Drabik had become more than an embarrassment. Anticipating the millennial year by a decade, Drabik proclaimed the coming of the thousand-year reign for the year 1656, which is the year also in which Comenius fled his home in ravaged Lezno for Amsterdam, and there prepared the sum of his pedagogical works for publication.

In the context of Drabik, the apparently innocent *Opera Didactica* were plans meant for immediate realization in a world soon to be wonderfully transformed [13].

---

[11] John Amos Comeinus, *On Education* (New York: Teachers College Press, 1967), pp. 35-64.

[12] Will-Erich Peuckert, *Das Rosenkreuz*, 2nd ed. (Berlin: Erich Schmidt Verlag), p. 181.

[13] To be fair to the Manuels, they fully recognize the «deep Christian millenarian roots of the utopia of expanding human capacities» and know that these «are annoying only to those who would translate

Comenius had long beet at the center of visionary reforms and, as early as 1630 he met a counterpart in Samuel Hartlib to whom later Milton would dedicate his essay *Of Education* (1644) [14]. Hartlib had already become acquainted with all the foundation documents of the Rosicrucians and sought out Comeinus for a manifesto. Comeinus delivered the *Didactica Magna* instead, far too practical to qualify as an introduction to the great Pansophia or to satisfy the circle around Hartlib, though, in Comenius's own terms it was probably meant as a map for education in the millennium. At the core of Hartlib's utopian plans (partly his own, partly those of his soul mate, John Drury) were the creation of a universal academy, the restoration of one faith (at least among Protestants), and the introduction of a universal language [15]. This has been an apocalyptic expectation for almost as long as there have been apocalyptic expectations: one common law will prevail over the world, one eternal government, one sacrifice, one worship, one people, and one language on the face of the earth [16]. At least one of Hartlib's plans was realized after the Restoration (and his discreet retirement) in the establishment of the Royal Society in which his friends, among them Robert Boyle, played important roles.

The History of Science has, with some incredulity on the part of practicing scientists, restored the importance of magic, the occult, and the esoteric to the story of the beginnings of modern science. Newton was, after all, an alchemist (and apocalypticist) before, during, and after the composition of the *Principia Mathematica*, and Newton, Locke, and Boyle (who banned alchemy from the agenda of the Royal Society), exchanged a serious alchemical correspondence, swearing one another to secrecy [17]. It would probably be well for the histo-

the rich Christian utopian corpus of Western society into purely secular terms» (p. 318f.).

[14] Charles Webster, ed., *Samuel Hartlib and the Advancement of Learning* (Cambridge: at the University Press, 1970), p. 2.

[15] Peuckert, *Rosenkreuz*, 2nd ed., pp. 185-91.

[16] «Sibylline Oracles», 3.746-780; «Testament of Judah», 25, 3-5: *Old Testament Pseudepigrapha*, ed. James H. Charlesworth (Garden City: Doubleday, 1983), 1, 378-79, 802.

[17] B. J. T. Dobbs, *The Foundation of Newton's Alchemy* (Cambridge: Cambridge University Press, 1975); R. S. Westfall, «Newton and Alchemy», *Occult and Scientific Mentalities in the Renaissance*,

rians and critics of Utopia similarly to remember the apocalyptic environment, both theoretical and practical, from which the modern Utopia sprang. It continues to inform Utopia in all its manifestations, even, or especially, those which most assiduously avoid or vociferously repudiate transcendent forces, those which alone would keep their envisioned paradises from turning in Big Rock Candy Mountains (or into nightmares).

Frank L. Borchardt
Duke University

---

ed. Brian Vickers (Cambridge: Cambridge University Press, 1984), p. 315; Frank E. Manuel, *The Religion of Isaac Newton* (Oxford: at the Clarendon Press, 1974).

CINEMATIC DEVICES IN THE CUBAN-FRENCH THEATRE OF EDUARDO MANET

There is no doubt that the relationship between theatre and film is symbiotic. The stage has given to the screen many of its most memorable texts. The screen, in turn, starting with silent films, has had a powerful influence on playwrights. In Spanish theatre, one need look no farther than the two major figures of the early twentieth century: Federico García Lorca and Ramón del Valle-Inclán. The influence may appear in a number of ways, direct and indirect. Lorca's *El paseo de Buster Keaton* makes a clear, intertextual reference to film. In his *esperpentos*, Valle-Inclán, somewhat more subtly, calls for visual images and a temporal-spatial fluidity that appeared «unstageable» at the time of their creation.

In the contemporary period, there are many examples of continued symbiosis. When film actor Fernando Fernán-Gómez turned to playwriting, it came as no surprise that the resulting *La bicicletas son para el verano* had a cinematic structure and that it could readily be transformed into one of Spain's most successful movies of the 1980s. Similarly one should not be surprised to find a strong element of popular culture in the works of Latin-America authors like Manuel Puig, who admits to being raised on Hollywood movies (Puig).

An excellent example of the relationship between film techniques and theatre is the work of Eduardo Manet. Born in Cuba in 1927, Manet studied theatre in Paris in the 1950s and has resided there permanently since 1968. He usually writes directly in French and is the Latin American author who has achieved the greatest success on the French stage (Obregón 37). The use of cinematic devices in his plays is intentional. When Manet originally left Havana, he had planned to study film but inadvertently arrived in Paris too late to register at the l'Institut des Hautes Etudes Cinématographiques and found himself in acting school instead. When he returned to Cuba in 1960 at Fidel Castro's invitation, he initially assumed the direction of the Cuban national theatre but then shifted to movie-making. Before he left Cuba again for exile in France, he had directed four feature-length and six short films, one of which, *El Negro*, won an international prize at a London festival (Mignon 6).

Manet's love of the movies, like Puig's dates back to childhood, when he recalls skipping school to watch Mae West, Greta Garbo, the Marx Brothers, and Chaplin. He sees a general impact of film on all the Hispanic stage directors and authors living in France: «Les enfants, les adolescents latino-américains on été littéralement nourris de cinéma américain. Demandez à Georges Lavelli, Severo Sarduy, Alfredo Arias, Jérôme Savary, tous vont vous parler de l'influence du cinéma américain dans leur travail» (Mambrino 361).

The cinematic influence on Manet appears in a variety of ways across his theatrical oeuvre, no matter what the theme or approach a particular text may take. It is present from his first major stage play, *Les Nonnes*, 1969, to his most recent works, both written in 1987: the historical *Juan y Teresa en busca de Dios* and the metaphorical *Les Chiennes*. Manet's characters are prone to metatheatrical games: role-playing within the role. Often the roles they assume are clear intertextual references to movies, and the lines they give themselves to speak are drawn from the discourse of film. The action typically reveals a cinematic structure in its temporalspatial fluidity, for example in the use of simultaneous action and flashbacks. While in the early plays, from *Les Nonnes* to *Lady Strass*, 1977, the setting is generally an enclosed space and the movement comes solely through the interaction of the characters and their role-playing, in several of the later works, such as *Un balcon sur les Andes* (1979), *Mendoza, en Argentina* (1983), and *Histoire de Maheu le boucher* (1986), the action moves to the outside and the text could readily be turned into a movie script.

The stage directions in both groups of plays often include film terminology, suggesting, for example, that the actors' movements simulate a freeze, slow motion, or the projection of frames at double speed. It should be noted that Manet has been in the forefront in this use of cinematic devices. Mireille Willey has identified Jorge Lavelli as an innovator for the the introduction in his staging of Arrabal's *Bella Ciao* at the Théâtre National Populaire in February 1972 of «le procédé du ralentio qui était jusqu'alors exploité exclusivement par le cinéma et la télévision» (32). Manet, however, had already expdicitly called for the varied rhythms of film in his *Eux ou La prise du pouvoir* the year before.

Also readily identifiable with film are Manet's use of such lighting techniques as fade-outs and fade-ins and, even more so, of music and sound. The latter may become a virtual soundtrack: drumbeats, or other sounds of revolution, or the menacing roar of the lions accompanied by the cheers of the crowd (*Les Nonnes: Madras, la nuit où...*, 1974; *Holocaustum ou le Borgne*, 1972). On occasion the soundtrack includes offstage voices, real or imagined (*Un balcon sur les Andes, Mendoza, en Argentina, Ma'Dèa*, 1984). Typically there is a pervasive background of shifting musical motifs. The music itself, like the roles the characters choose for their metatheatrical games, may refer to the old Hollywood movies, and the sounds of American movies crop up in the most unexpected places. Even *L'autre Don Juan*, Manet's play-within-a-play staging of Juan Ruiz de Alarcón's seventeenth-century *Las paredes oyen*, makes use of a «bande de son très riche d'un film de l'Ouest américain: henissements des chevaux, roues qui s'arrêtent avec un bruit énorme, etc.» (86).

Although all of Manet's theatre is self-consciously metatheatrical, the deliberate acting, out of film images by the characters within the play is nowhere more obvious than in *Eux ou La prise du pouvoir*. Staged by the Comédie Française at the Petit Odéon in 1971, the play is intended to be performed without an intermission — yet another device that relates it to film. In their ritualistic game playing, Monsieur and Madame Arthur assume a number of roles. Wearing a blond wig, she appears initially as a Hollywood vamp of the 30s (14); her gestures are to be vaguely reminiscent of Garbo or Swanson (19). With a change of hair and costume, she later becomes Ava Gardner of *The Barefoot Contessa* (10). He at one point adopts the voice and facial expressions of Jerry Lewis (43); at another he pulls out a revolver and spins it, «comme les cow-boys du cinéma» (83). Stage directions continually underscore the influence of film. Monsieur Arthur interrupts his singing, in English, of «Happy Birthday», stops short, and stares at Madame Arthur «comme l'image fixe d'un film» (14). In a frantic, comic moment, Monsieur Arthur pushes a small player piano around the stage while Madame Arthur attempts to keep a serving cart out of his reach: the scene is to evoke «un mouvement de cinéma muet» (22).

Manet's film images may be less explicit elsewhere than in *Eux ou La prise du pouvoir* but are often used with greater dramatic impact. To illustrate his creative integration of cinema into theatre, I have chosen the example of *Lady Strass*. Stage by Roger Blin at the Théâtre de Poche Montparnasse in 1977, it is one of several Manet texts in which role-playing assumes psychological and sociological meaning. By the end of this baroque psychodrama, the three characters have gone beyond the series of stereotypical images they portray both to take on a life of their own and to reflect, through the cultures they represent, the relative decadence of old Europe and the vitality of Latin America.

The central character of *Lady Strass* is an eccentric older Englishwoman who has barricaded herself in a house in Belize; shut off from the outside world and the danger of political unrest in Central America, she is free to live in an imagined past. When two would-be thieves break into her isolated, boarded-up house, they find themselves trapped inside and confronted by the rifle-toting lady, dressed in Western garb. Bertrand, a middle-aged Frenchman, and the younger Manuel, a mestizo from Guatemala, are thus obliged to enter into Mrs. Eliane Parkington Simpson's theatricalized life.

The play is explicitly metatheatrical. The room that forms the set indeed has a stage and a balcony. When the two men first illuminate it with their flashlights, Manuel says it looks like a church. Bertrand corrects him: «Non. Un théâtre» (10). Eliane later produces a variety of costumes which she says remain from the amateur theatricals she and her second husband used to stage. But the melodramatic stories she tells of her two marriages, her life in India and Belize, and her tragic love stories are all reminiscent of films, as is her own hybrid image of an eccentric British aristocrat with a touch of Annie Oakley. The first words she speaks, over loudspeakers at that,

40

are pure Hollywood: «Don't move! Ne bougez pas! No se muevan! You are under surveillance! Estais siendo vigilados!» (10). When she later asserts her loyalty to England and her sharpshooting skills, the lines juxtapose two distinct intertextual references to film: «Là où il y a un anglais et une anglaise au coeur vaillant, l'Empire Britannique existe et existera dans toute sa gloire. Sachez, en plus, que je fais mouche sur une boîte d'allumette à cent pas. A la prochaine insulte, je vous descends» (12).

Manuel, dressed up for a party in the costume Eliane has provided, overtly evokes a film image. Bertrand says he looks like «Fred-je-ne-sais-pas-quoi» from an American movie he saw in Tegucigalpa (18). Later in the scene, the stage directions indicate that Manuel is to look «plus "Valentino" que jamais» (20). Although not explicitly a film image, Manuel's subsequent unexpected appearance as a Nazi officer is likewise drawn from the movies. The German uniform Manuel has found in a closet would be familiar to Manet himself and to most spectators, not directly through memories of World War II, but indirectly through the cinematic portrayal of the period. The same is true of «Lili Marlène», the musical background that accompanies Manuel in his new role as Hans.

In *Lady Strass* there is an almost constant use of music, ranging from *Tristan and Isolde* by Wagner to a flute from India. In the central scenes of the play, when the characters evoke the parties of Eliane's remembered or imagined past, the music is readily associated with movies: «Ramona», «Smoke Gets in Your Eyes», a «charleston genre *Gold Diqqers 1933*» (20). The effects created by this background music, alternately sentimental and lighthearted, are important to the development of the action. Eliane at the beginning of the play is a delightful eccentric, an almost comic combination of two contrasting film stereotypes. In the party scene, she is still the aristocrat, but a vivacious one who teaches Bertrand to dance. In the final scenes of the play, when Manuel forces her to confront the sordid truth of her past, she retreats to madness. The dramatic impact of the ending is dependent upon the change in Eliane's character.

A revival of *Lady Strass* in Fall 1987 at the Théâthe Marie-Stuart in Paris highlighted the importance of Manet's cinematic intertextuality — by eliminating it. Perhaps because of budget restraints, perhaps because of the director's unfamiliarity with the references, the production did away with Eliane's Western garb and guns, with her elegant pre-World War I gown in the party scene, and with Manuel's dressing up as Valentino. It likewise replaced «Smoke Gest in Your Eyes» and the charleston with indistinguishable, loud contemporary music. The dance became violent instead of funny. All the intertextual humor or the early scenes had disappeared. Rather than have Eliane degenerate from eccentricity to madness, with concommitant changes in linguistic registers, she simply reflected a monochord madness throughout. Bertrand's gallant French gesture, his apparent decision to stay with her and care for her, became inexplicable. Additionally, in losing its series of historical allusions evoked through film images, the play also lost its subtextual message: its implicit criticism of Western materialism and imperialism, including cultural imperialism, as exemplified by various nations in the course of the twentieth century.

The richness of Manet's theatre is dependent upon cinematic devices and film images both for its brilliant technical effects and for its implicit ideology. To ignore these aspects of his work is to impoverish it. The intertextual references to old Hollywood movies, however, should not be lost upon a younger generation of theatre people and spectators. Those same Hollywood films lurk in the background of the Spanish theatre of the 1980s, the works of the so-called New New Authors or Hyperrealists (José Luis Alonso de Santos, Fermín Cabal, Sebastián Junyent), who readily admit their addiction to the late-late movies on TV. The influence of Hollywood film images on contemporary world theatre is not likely to disappear soon. The theatre of Eduardo Manet will therefore remain a fascinating example of a major current of the legitimate stage.

Phyllis Zatlin
Rutgers University

WORKS CITED

Mambrino, Jean: «Entretien avec... Eduardo Manet», *Revue Etudes*, March 1985: 359-374.

Manet, Eduardo: *Les Nonnes*, Paris: Gallimard, 1969.

—: *Eux ou La prise du pouvoir*, Paris: Gallimard, 1971.

—: *Holocaustum ou le Borgne*, Paris: Gallimard, 1972.

—: *L'autre Don Juan*, Paris: Gallimard, 1973.

—: *Madras, la nuit où...*, Paris: Gallimard, 1975.

—: *Lady Strass. L'Avant-Scéne Théâtre*, 613 (1 July 1977): 5-31.

—: *Un balcon sur les Andes, Mendoza, en Argentine..., Ma'Déa*, Paris: Gallimard, 1985.

—: *Histoire de Maheu le boucher*, Paris: Gallimard, 1986.

—: *Les Chiennes*, Tapuscrit 47, Paris: Théâtre Ouvert, 1987.

—: *Juan y Teresa en busca de Dios*, Unpublished typescript, 1987.

—: Personal interview, 19 October 1987.

Mignon, Paul-Louis: «Le théâtre de A jusqu'à Z: Eduardo Manet», *L'Avant-Scéne Théâtre*, 613 (1 July 1977), 6-7.

Obregón, Osvaldo: «Apuntes sobre el teatro latinoamericano en Francia», *Cahiers du Monde Hispanique et Luso-Brésilien*, 40 (1983), 17-45.

Puig, Manuel: A Dialogue with Manuel Puig and Literary Critics. Barnard College, New York City, 9 April 1987.

Willey, Mireille: *«"Théâtres populaires" d'aujourd-hui en France et en Angleterre (1960-1975). Etude comparative*, Paris: Dider-Erudition, 1979.

ILIAD 6.242-250 AND *ODYSSEY* 14.5-17: PARODY OR PARADIGM?

The description of the piggery in *Odyssey* 14.5-17 has been characterized as «almost a parody» of Priam's palace in *Iliad* 6.242-50 [1]. While the implied comparison between the extended family of an oriental monarch and the teeming pens of a humble swineherd is quite amusing, it is possible that the similarity between the two passages is more than just humorous [2]. In an orally-composing tradition, from which the *Iliad* and the *Odyssey* undoubtedly derive, poets often employ the same groups of ideas to narrate a repeated scene such as arming for battle, preparing a meal, or gathering for assembly. The specific details mentioned in any given theme may vary, with some features now present, now absent, but the basic pattern of ideas remains [3]. In *Il.* 6 and *Od.* 14, the repetition of many of the same ideas establishes that the two passages are alternative realizations of the same theme. They both contain a father-figure (Priam, Eumaeus), a house built of dressed stones (*Il.* 6.244 ξεστοιο λιθοιο, *Od.* 14.9 ρυτοισιν λαεσσι), numerous inhabitants (children in the *Iliad*, pigs in the *Odys-*

---

[1] D. B. Monro, *Homer's Odyssey*, Books XIII-XXIV (Oxford, 1901), commentary ad loc.

[2] Norman Austin suggests that the digressions in the *Iliad* are «both thematically and dramatically ... relevant to the structure of the whole poem», in his article «The Function of Digressions in the *Iliad*», reprinted in *Essays on the Iliad*, ed. John Wright (Indiana, 1978), p. 71.

[3] Albert Lord, *The Singer of Tales* (New York, 1974), p. 68, defines a theme as «the groups of ideas regularly used in telling a tale in the formulaic style of traditional song». On typical scenes, see Walter Arend, *Die Typische Scenen bei Homer* (Berlin, 1933), and Bernard Fenik, *Typical Battle Scenes in the Iliad* (Wiesbaden, 1968).

sey), rooms close to one another (πλησιον αλληλων in both), and groups of 50 and 12 (50 sons and daughters-in-law and 12 daughters and sons-in-law in the *Iliad*, 12 pigsties with 50 pigs each in the *Odyssey*). This paper argues that the theme embodied in these two passages conveys an important underlying message about the relationship of domestic order to the well-being of society in archaic Greece.

The description of Priam's palace forms part of the *Iliad*'s meditation on one of its most important themes, the nature of domestic and civilized life in the eighth-century *polis*. In his discussion of *Il.* 6.242-50, Schein notes that «the beauty and sophistication of the architecture, combined with Homer's emphasis on the sleeping arrangements of Priam's children and their spouses, show Troy to be a center of civilized refinement and domestic decorum». Troy is «a city that represents all that is domestically and socially most humane and civilized — a city much like the home cities the Greek warriors left behind» [4]. The central image in *Il.* 6.242-250 is the picture of husbands and wives peacefully lying side-by-side in groups of fity and twelve under the roof of the great *paterfamilias* (6.246, 250). This picture contrasts strongly with the illicit and inappropriate relationship of Helen and Paris in *Il.* 3.373-461. Not only do they have intercourse when Paris should be fighting, but their unauthorized «marriage» is the cause of the entire war. The idea that inappropriate sexual relations threaten the existence of a whole community finds expression in several other scenes in the *Iliad*. Agamemnon's attempt to take the daughter of a priest as his concubine results in the plagues of Book 1. When he takes the concubine properly allotted to Achilles as reparation for the loss of Chryseis, a series of crises and disasters ensues. A concern for the societal consequences of sexual relationships is at the heart of the plot of the *Iliad*, which provides a picture of both the proper (Priam's family except for Paris, Hector and Andromache, Achilles and Briseis) and the improper (Paris and Helen, Agamemnon and Chryseis, Agamemnon and Briseis). The disastrous effects of improper relations are clearly portrayed, including the destruction of the town and civilization of Troy.

---

[4] Seth Schein, *The Mortal Hero* (California, 1984), pp. 169-70.

The same message is central to the *Odyssey*. In Odysseus' own home there is no possibility of a direct comparison between proper and improper households such as Priam's many offspring provide, since Telemachus is an only child. But the theme of a large household with many children under a father's protection actually appears three times in the *Odyssey*, in different guises: Eumaeus' pigsty at *Od.* 14.5-17, where it is most fully developed; Polyphemus' dwelling in 9.181-239; and the brief scene of the serving maids of Odysseus at 22.421-24. The similarities of Eumaeus' piggery to Priam's palace have been noted above, but the role of the father-figure is emphasized in the case of Eumaeus, for he appears as a benevolent parent to more than just his animals. He plays the role of father to both Odysseus and Telemachus. Telemachus calls Eumaeus «daddy» (αττα) six times, but never bestows this childish epithet on Odysseus, even after he learns his identity. When Telemachus returns to Ithaca from his voyages, he makes first for the hut of the swineherd, where he is received «as a father welcomes his only grown son» (16.17-19). When Odysseus finally arrives on Ithaca, he strangely seeks help not from his own father Laertes, but from Eumaeus. The Polyphemus passage is less central to the message about sex and society and will not be discussed in detail here, but it is worth noting that Polyphemus is not a good model for an important message about Greek society, because the Cyclopes are described as having no society and not living like human beings (*Od.* 9.106-115) [5]. His home does however provide a useful background of ordinary pasturing routine against which to view the significance of the structure of Eumaeus' homestead. Finally, the serving maids of Odysseus,

---

[5] Polyphemus' cave has an αυλη of stones buried in the earth (185-6 περι δ' αυλη / υψηλη δεδμητο κατωρυχεεσσι λιθοισι) plus a wooden enclosure, like Eumaeus' yard (Polyphemus: 9.186; Eumaeus: 14.11-12), while Priam's home boasts an αυλη of polished stones. Both Eumaeus and Polyphemus are heads of large households, as is Priam: Eumaeus tends swine while Polyphemus is the guardian of multitudinous flocks of sheep and goats. Polyphemus' home is similar in some ways to the other homesteads because the methods of composition in Greek epic encouraged such thematic similarity, but the absence of the numbers twelve and fifty suggests that this home does not fall into the structural pattern of the others, and does not communicate the same message.

mentioned in 22.421-24 as being fifty in number, provide the only indication of heroic proportions in Odysseus' household. Twelve have stooped to sleeping with the suitors, an obvious connection with the children of Priam and the sows of Eumaeus, bot hof whom sleep in groups of fifty and twelve. These passages, *Il.* 6.242-250, *Od.* 14.5-7 and 22.421-424, are the only instances in epic of the juxtaposition of the numbers fifty and twelve, and it is likely that they also share a similar message [6]. Each of these three passages stresses different aspects of the theme, and in combination they develop and deepen its message. The less exalted stature of the *Odyssey*'s households, particularly the humble setting of Eumaeus' homestead and the rustic cave of Polyphemus, represents a transposition of the idea of the necessity of domestic order to a stable society from Priam's palace to the realm of the Greek householder listening to the poem [7]. The *Odyssey* appears from this perspective to be a detailed commentary on archaic Greek social mores, with perhaps a bit of moralizing thrown in.

Separation by sex is the most important difference between the Iliadic and Odyssean versions of this theme. Eumaeus' boars sleep outside, apart from the females as do Polyphemus' male animals (*Od.* 9.237-39). In the case of Polyphemus this is no more than normal farming practice, but the sleeping arrangements of Eumaeus' pigs signal the necessary state of domestic order on Ithaca, namely, that male and female must be separated as long as Odysseus is away. The passage also emphasizes the sexual basis of such order, which the fate of the serving maids in *Od.* 22 bears out. The difference in sleeping arrangements is not due simply to the different plots and settings of the two poems. On Ithaca, social norms are in danger of collapsing as the reckless suitors pursue Penelope. Penelope's lawful husband is away, and her sexual segregation from the suitors is essential if Odysseus' *oikos* is to survive. Thus Penelope huddles, penned in her *thalamos* like a fertile sow [8], carefully separated from all males. Penelope stays far

---

[6] In contrast, Polyphemus's animals are divided into threes, and the numbers twelve and fifty do not occur.

[7] My thanks to Norman Austin for suggesting this idea to me. Note also that Eumaeus is, like Priam, of royal birth, the only one of Odysseus' servants to hold such a distinction (Od. 15.413-4).

[8] Cf. the simile with which Odysseus greets his wife, *Od.* 109-114, stressing her fertility.

from the suitors, dangerous men who consume the pigs of Eumaeus until they are finally butchered like the animals they devoured. They represent sexual danger, since they spend every waking hour near Penelope, dreaming of making love to her (18.213). Even Penelope's son, Telemachus, sleeps in a *thalamos* clearly situated outside the domestic part of the house, and nowhere near Penelope's sleeping quarters [9]. Odysseus' fortunes depend on Penelope's sexual fidelity (but sometimes his own lack of fidelity, as in the Circe passage). In the *Iliad*, both Paris and Helen are guilty of destroying the city of Troy, although Helen's crime is the worse because she betrays her husband. In the *Odyssey*, Penelope's marriage to one of the suitors would destroy the household and lineage of Odysseus, much as Clytemnestra's alliance with Aegisthus nearly wipes out Agamemnon's legitimate inheritors [10]. Despite Penelope's constant faithfulness, Odysseus contemplates the possibility that his wife is capable of such an act at 13.383-4, and Athena warns Telemachus about the consequences of Penelope's so doing at 15.20-23. Penelope is clearly depicted in the *Odyssey* as a potential Helen or Clytemnestra.

The need to express the grave danger to the *oikos* arising from the sexual separation of Penelope and Odysseus under-

---

[9] Dorothea Gray, «Houses in the*Odyssey*», CQ n.s.5 (1955), 1-12, places Telemachus' *thalamos* at some distance from the megaron and Penelope's quarters. It may be that unmarried sons normally slept in the αι'θουσα until they married, at which time they received their own *thalamos* or moved to a separate house (compare Peisistratus, Od. 3.399, who sleeps beside Telemachus in the porch while Nestor and his wife sleep μυχω δομου υψηλοιο, 402), but this does not lessen the effect of the poet's emphatic separation between the sleeping quarters of mother and son.

Laertes, who might be expected to provide some assistance to his beleaguered daughter-in-law, lives εκ πολιος (24.205) and never comes near to help her.

[10] Marilyn B. Arthur, «Early Greece: The Origins of the Western Attitude Toward Women», in *Women in the Ancient World: the Arethusa Papers*, ed. John Peradotto and J. P. Sullivan (Albany, 1984). pp. 22-4, discusses this topic, but feels that it is not until the time of Hesiod that women exhibit the power to damage the social order with their sexuality. Jasper Griffin in *Homer. The Odyssey* (Cambridge, 1987), pp. 87-89, observes that although it is ambigous whether the kingship of Ithaca follows Penelope or not, the logic of the poem demands that Odysseus be depicted as about to lose everything: wife, possessions, kingdom.

lies the emphasis on the sleeping arrangements of Eumaeus' «children», which corresponds to the emphasis on Priam's children's sleeping quarters in the *Iliad* noted by Schein above. The sows of Eumaeus lie in their beds, ευνας συσιν, sleeping on the ground, χαμαιευναδες. The emphasis on beds in the description of the piggery makes little sense in that context, but heightens its power to illuminate social mores in the human realm by hinting that the crux of the connections between the house of Priam, the pigsties, and Odysseus' situation is in the possible sexual relations that occur in bed. The boars, who are carefully separated from the sows, lie (ιαυον) outside. The verb ιαυον denotes having sexual relations at *Od*. 22.464, and may retain that association in 14.16. In contrast, the children of Priam κοιμωντο side by side, sleeping side-by-side in the protective and protected bonds of matrimony.

The shared marriage bed is a central image in each poem, but especially in the *Odyssey*, where it signifies both the relationship between Penelope and Odysseus and the security of the community on Ithaca. When Penelope refuses to believe that Odysseus has really returned to Ithaca, he immediately demands that a bed be made up for him in the megaron (23.171-2). Penelope counters by suggesting he sleep just outside their old *thalamos* (23.177-8). Odysseus then describes their unique marriage bed (23.190-201), which convinces Penelope to accept the stranger as her own husband. As she does so, she reminds Odysseus that she is nothing like Helen, a woman who abused her marriage bed and destroyed Troy. Only 200 lines later the audience hears Agamemnon's tale of treachery at the hands of his wife Clytemnestra, a betrayal that nearly cost the house of Atreus possession of the throne. Penelope is really telling Odysseus that her sexual fidelity has ensured the safety of society on Ithaca in his absence.

The passage from *Od*. 22 further reinforces the connection of the theme of the large household with a message about sex and society. Here Telemachus is about to punish the serving-maids who have shown their unfaithfulness to Odysseus by sleeping with Penelope's suitors. At *Od*. 22.420-24, Eurycleia tells Telemachus that of the fifty maids in the house, twelve have gone in for shamelessness. He kills them because they have lain with (ιαυον) the suitors (22.464). The numbers twelve and fifty, plus the use of the verb ιαυον, link this passage with the others and allow the message to be stated explicitly. The maids have slept with the suitors during the time it was dangerous to society for male and female to sleep together, and their punishment must be a painful death.

The similarity in images and theme between the palace of Priam and the pigsty of Eumaeus, otherwise so different, shows that the underlying message of both passages is that society is in danger when sexual norms are flouted. In both poems, extramarital relations threaten the emerging social structure of archaic Greece. It may be that the Iliadic passage was composed earlier, and provided a paradigm which the poet(s) of the *Odyssey* further developed to make an unmistakable point. That female sexuality is particularly dangerous is made clear in the Odyssean passages: females must be penned, for when they escape the control of the *oikos*, as the serving maids do, disaster is sure to follow [11].

Julie Williams
Lehigh University

[11] Eumaeus' nursemaid was persuaded to sell him into slavery after an illicit affair with a Phoenician trader (*Od.* 15.415-453).

THE DELPHIC DILEMMA IN STENDHAL'S
VIE DE HENRY BRULARD

«Mais combien ne faut-il pas de précautions
pour ne pas mentir!»

(Stendhal, 33.)

From the moment he decides to «write his life», Stendhal confronts the constitutive questions governing 19th-century autobiography: Who am I? Who was I in the past? How has my present self evolved? And which events have most significantly contributed to this development? All of these have to do with the problem of identity and the relationship of the subject to his text. They serve to both focus the writer on his task and to promote the movement of the text in a specific direction.

As the above questions suggest Stendhal, no less than other writers of conventional autobiographies, is motivated by a desire for unity, for the integral self or, as Louis Marin has it, by a desire to «mend with a pen the tissue of his life torn into pieces, so as to make the "I-as-I" and the "I-as-he" coincide» (887). Conventional autobiography, as Stendhal knew it, promises to replace the multiple, discontinuous referential selves of empirical reality with the coherent, continuous, figural self of the autobiographic text. His introspective reflection, «il serait bien temps de me connaître» (28) in the beginning, is nothing other than a manifestation of the longing for such a synthesizing ideal, a self which can ultimately be reduced to a single denominator and find its proper place within a given social, cultural, and political order. This is the teleological goal of conventional autobiography, the ideal toward which all of its elements pertaining to form and content tend to gravitate.

At the beginning of the text, Stendhal is not fully aware that this goal will in fact always be beyond his reach; it is one of the important discoveries he will make, *peu à peu* in the very process of remembering and writing as he becomes increasingly aware of the need to supplement memory with the constitutive language of narration.

Whereas a modernist autobiography consciously places the reader squarely within this self-reflexive and constitutive process of writing, Stendhal's text arrives at such insights either belatedly or accidentally in that they are engendered by the spontaneity of the act of writing, rather than the result of deliberate, conscious reflection[1]. Indeed the idea of writing an autobiography seems to come about by chance; it is the consequence of a series of reflections and associations preceding the beginning of the actual recollections. Situated on *le mont Janicule,* far above the center of city, Stendhal looks down upon the traces of ancient and modern history in the form of monuments, ruins, tombs, aqueducts, streets and gardens. The contemplation of this multi-layered tableau inaugurates a chain of mental associations and responses that will ultimately lead to the conception of the autobiographic project. As he surveys the panorama of Rome, his glance eventually lands upon the old convent on Mount Albano which had been, he recalls, the home of Raphael's famous painting, the «Transfiguration», for *two-hundred and fifty years.* This bit of art history serves as reminder that he will soon be *fifty* years old and that he still does not know who he is: «Ah! dans trois mois j'aurai *cinquante ans,* estil bien possible!» «... il serait bien temps de me connaître» (28, my emphasis).

In subsequently thinking about the painting in its present location, Stendhal obliquely alludes to the act of remembering as a visual and fallible event. This definition will govern his conception of remembering and writing throughout the remainder of the text.

Removed from its original premise, Raphael's painting now in its crypt-like setting, remains hidden from public view

---

[1] Stendhal allows the text to flow from his pen without interruption. He himself confirms this when he states, «En moins d'une heure, je viens d'écrire ces douze pages» (212), and «13 pages en une heure et demie», *Vie de Henry Brulard* (480). He finished the entire manuscript in less than four months.

«au fond du Vatican» (28), much as many impressions of the past lie buried and «ruined» [2] beyond the reach of conscious perception, in a distant corner of the psyche. In addition, the name of the painting, the «Transfiguration» suggests the process by which the incomplete, indistinct and silent visual images of the past are figuratively transformed into the more concrete, more enduring marks of writing. In the process Stendhal will coincidentally discover the truth about writing and remembering, a discover which will eventually result in his abandoning the impossible quest for self-knowledge and its related search for «truth» in favor of the consciously fictional and therefore philosophically less complicated modes of self representation, *La Chartreuse de Parme*.

Like Freud's return of the repressed, the question of identity repeatedly rises to the surface of the text in various forms and disguises, especially in the beginning: «Qu'ai-je été, que suis-je, en vérité, je serais bien embarassé de le dire (28). Qu'ai-je donc été? Je ne le saurais» (29). At first Stendhal naively assumes that these questions will perhaps be answered when his project is completed, in two to three years: «je saurai peut-être enfin, quand cela sera fini dans deux ou trois ans, ce que j'ai été, gai ou triste, homme d'esprit ou sot, homme de courage ou peureux, et enfin au total heureux ou malheureux...» (30). This statement constitutes the fragile foundation of personal attributes upon which Stendhal hopes to fasten his ever elusive identity.

As a figures for sameness, identity reduces diversity; it filters out deviations and differences from the object it attempts to name. And by foreclosing the possibility of the coincidence of a term and its opposite, it directs and predetermines the potential answer to the question «Who am I?». In other words, in orden to fix his identity, Stendhal must choose between happy and sad, courageous and cowardly, hypocritical and sincere, for within the ideology of identity, in contrast to our experience in the real world, it is impossible to at the same time be one and the other. The moment we admit the simultaneous existence of these opposite qualities, we displace the ideology of identity, uniqueness, singleness and sameness with the subversive conception of a subject

---

[2] I borrow this particular use of the word from Eugene Donato.

based on multiplicity, diversity and difference, a conception of the self defined by what Stendhal calls «cette effroyable quantité de Je et de Moi» (30), whose dissonant voices threaten to mutilate, disrupt and rupture the desired coherence of the text. The simulated chronological break of three years [3] that follows this discovery hyperbolically figures the reflective pause engendered by the writer's confrontation with the problematic of the multiple selves in relationship to writing and remembering [4].

In his second attempt to write, Stendhal hopes to avoid the conflict between the multiple selves and identity by simply yielding to what he calls the pleasure of writing — «Je trouve quelque fois beaucoup de plaisir à écrire, voilà tout» (31) only to find himself tempted by self-examination. This, however, constitutes yet another approach to the question, «Who am I», with which the text originally began. And for a 19th century text intending to be an autobiography, how could it be otherwise? The question is necessary for the production of the text. Its ever elusive answer opens the theoretical space in which it becomes possible for conventional autobiography to write itself. To stop asking it means nothing short of abandoning the text altogether. Not until the myth of the unified subject is definitively displaced by the myth of the multiple selves, can autobiography come into being without its inaugurating question and shift its emphasis to the spectacle of the dissolution and the reconstitution of the subject at the moment of writing.

The search for truth, simply another attempt to reduce the subject to a specific identity, proves to be no less problematic than the quest for self. Stendhal's passion «pour arriver au vrai» (40) derives from the belief the self can "present" itself "authentically and truthfully" if the writer only takes care to conscientiously and sincerely record the significant events of his life, even at the risk of presenting himself in a light, less

---

[3] For a summary of the biographical details surrounding the conception and actual production of this work, see Philippe Lejeune, «Stendhal et les problème autobiographiques» (28). Also see Louis Marin, «The Autobiographical Interruption» (617).

[4] Gérard Genette points out such spaces, blanks or breaks in Stendhal's text, are never meaningless, never simple absences but «une manque actif et sensible comme manque, comme inécriture, comme texte inécrit» (176).

desirable than he may wish. More specifically, for Stendhal telling the truth means avoiding the temptation to fictionalize, a temptation he finds virtually impossible to resist almost from the moment he begins to write. Shortly after declaring he will write «sans mentir j'espère, sans me faire illusion» (32), we are told that he had been a soldier at Wagram in 1809; only half a page later the text declares that this was not so (33). The amusing alibi, «quarante-cinq ans avant il était de mode d'avoir été soldat sous Napoléon» (33), hardly justifies this transgression into the realm of fiction if one expects autobiography to guarantee the referential bond between textual and empirical reality.

Somewhat later Stendhal recollects one of the tempestuous encounters between the aunt he most detested, *la tante* Séraphie's and the young Henri. In a moment of childish contempt, the latter had graced the entry way to the family dining room with a caricature of his sister, Zénaïde, bearing the inscription «Caroline-Zénaïde B., rapporteuse» (130). Stendhal's celebrated verve is particularly evident in the staging of this amusing scene. It is modeled upon one of his favorite metaphors, a series of military advances and retreats, and to lend it credibility, it is supplemented by a schematic sketch depicting the movements of the parties involved. In spite of this figurative excess there is no doubt that, at the moment of its telling, the scene intends to be a mimetic account of an actual childhood event. It is therefore all the more surprising when upon its completion, the text deliberately undermines its own credibility with the narrators unsettling question», «Je m'interroge depuis une heure pour savoir si cette scène est bien vraie, réelle, ainsi que vingt autres qui, évoquées des ombres, reparaissent un peu, après des années d'oubli» (131).

This textual strategy, that is the affirmation of an event followed by questioning its truth value, is paradigmatic for Stendhal's treatment of the act recollection. Remembering begins with a «scopic» [5] moment, an imperfect visual event, or in Stendhal's language, a fresco rising to the surface of conscious perception from which time has erased significant por-

---

[5] Term borrowed from Louis Marin, «Bodies and Signs in Autobiography» (889).

tions («C'est toujours comme les fresques du [Campo Santo] de Pise où l'on aperçoit fort bien un bras, et le morceau d'à coté que representait la tête est tombé» [187]). While Stendhal does not explicitly analyze the conceptual consequences of this iconographic representation of memory, these are, as it were, performed by the text itself: numerous episodes are denied, corrected, or contradicted; the narrator arrives at the insight that cognition depends on hermeneutics in that given situations are understoood only after the fact and he recognizes that the proportions of visual impressions are modified by time and space. The implications for truth in remembering are clear. Memory is at best an imperfect instrument for putting us in touch with the past. As a partially-erased fresco, it ironically entails the means to subvert its own truth in that it embodies the lack that must and will inevitably be supplemented by the language of fiction. If there is truth, the text as a whole seems to say, it must be sought / thought in the ruins of the mental image, between the visible and the invisible, between the manifest and the repressed-somewhere above, below or between the lines of the written text.

If memory can neither produce nor guarantee the truth of the self, perhaps science can. «A force de classer mes amis de jeunesse par genres, comme M. Adrien de Jussieu fait pour ses plantes (en botanique)», the narrator speculates, «je cherche à atteindre cette vérité qui me fuit» (43-44). This first scientific attempt to capture the truth never gets beyond the intent to establish a taxonomy which immediately digresses into a series of reflections regarding the relativity of perception [6]. Another time Stendhal attempts to classify the women in his life (no less than twelve) according to some of their personal attributes and qualities. After quickly filing seven under the headings the richest, the poorest, the most spirited, and the most sublime, he impatiently skips over the remaining

---

[6] Stendhal arrives at the conclusion that perception is relative rather than constant by comparing the visual impressions he recollects from his childhood with those of his adult life: «Je m'aperçois que ce que je prenais pour de hautes montagnes, en 1800, n'étaient la plupart que des taupinières; mais c'est une découverte que je n'ai faite que bien tard» (44).

five, and impulsively yields to a subject of perhaps even greater importance, the role of money in his life [7].

With this playful, aborted, pseudo-scientific approach to the truth, «cette vérité qui... [lui] fuit» (43-44), Stendhal ironizes his own quest for the impossible and generally mocks man's impulse to order and classify observable reality according to mathematical tables and scientific charts in an attempt to reduce the question of truth to a calculable series of facts and figures. And to take this one step further, one might justifiably add that the scientific method, in spite of its arrogant pretensions, has no greater claim to any kind of constant, reliable truth regarding the nature and/or composition of the self than introspection, remembering and writing, its less rigorous, more open-ended companions.

Stendhal's text succeeds precisely because it fails. It fails in the task it has set for itself, the quest for truth and self-knowledge. The Delphic injunction, «[...] je ne prétends nullement écrire une histoire, mais tout simplement noter mes souvenirs afin de deviner quel homme j'ai été: bête ou spirituel, peureux ou courageux, etc. C'est la réponse au grand mot: Gnoti seauton» (216), remains unanswered — «Mais au fond, cher lecteur, je ne sais pas ce que je suis: bon, méchant, spirituel, sot» (280) — and the truth, as it was originally envisioned, always beyond apprehension. *Vie de Henry Brulard* thus estraddles the theoretical space that separates the unified, autonomous subject from the fragmented, determined self, and absolute, undeniable truth from multiplicity and relativity. As such it traces the shift in perception from consonance to dissonance, from coherence to incoherence, from continuity to discontinuity, in short, from the traditional to the modernist literary text.

Ingrid Stipa
St. Lawrence University

---

[7] Such digressions are characteristic of Stendhal's text. As Béatrice Didier notes, «La découverte que fait Stendhal à chaque page, c'est qu'il doit suivre l'ordre de la mémoire, non l'ordre du temps (227).

WORKS CITED

Didier, Beatrice: «Roman et Autobiographie», *Revue d'Histoire Littéraire de la France*, 2 (1984), 217-230.

Donato, Eugene: «The Ruins of Memory: Archaeological Fragments and Textual Artifacts», *Modern Language Notes*, 93 (1978), 575-596.

Genette, Gérard: «Stendhal», in *Figures II*, Paris: Le Seuil, 1968.

Lejeune, Philippe: «Stendhal et les problèmes de l'autobiographie», *Stendhal et les problèmes de l'autobiographie*, Ed. Victor del Litto, Grenoble: PU, 1976.

Marin, Louis: «Bodies and Signs in Autobiographie: Stendhal's *Life of Henry Brulard*», *Modern Language Notes*, 99 (1984), 887-998.

— «The Autobiographical Interruption: About Stendhal's *Life of Henry Brulard*», *Modern Language Notes*, 93 (1978): 597-617.

Stendhal, *Vie de Henry Brulard*, Ed. Béatrice Didier, Paris: Gallimard, 1973.

OBSERVATIONS AS TO THE ROLE OF
CENSORSHIP IN RECENT GDR PROSE

The fact that all literary publications in the GDR have been subject to the scrutiny and final approval by the Ministry of Culture had a significant impact on the literary development of that country. One obvious result was that quite a number of writers left the GDR — not all of them voluntarily — and now reside in the West, such as Sarah Kirsch, Jurek Becker, Rainer Kunze, Erich Löst, and Wolf Biermann. Very few established authors, such as Stefan Heym, have been publishing only in the West. Others, especially from among the very young generation, have gone underground and, of course, there is no way of knowing, how many works were never published nor how many potential authors never wrote because of the existing state censorship.

In this paper we shall focus paradigmatically on some of the major fictional writings from the last twenty years, in order to substantiate the thesis that censorship did not just have a negative impact on GDR literary production but that, on the contrary, it might also at times have stimulated the artistic genius. Indeed, some authors showed extraordinary skill, ingenuity, and artistic innovation in an effort to express their real concerns while, at the same time, trying to circumvent certain state restriction and conform — at least to some degree — to the expectation imposed by the mandates of the prevailing literary theory, i.e., Socialist Realism. Those efforts ultimately contributed in a significant way to the quality and sophistication of their works.

The artistic independence and self-confidence necessary for this kind of writing started to evolve in the early 1960's, with Christa Wolf's *Der geteilte Himmel* [1] Wanting to deal with topics like the division of Germany, population loss to the West, and even suicide — topics which so far had been more or less taboo in GDR literature —, Wolf had to devise a style of writing that would be wide open to interpretation if she wanted to have a chance for publication in her own country. That is to say, Wolf had to cope with delicate issues in such a way that favorably disposed critics would have the option to write interpretations which would satisfy the official demand of the prevailing literary doctrine [2]. The ensuing critical debate and controversy in both East and West, resulting in a lengthy summary volume [3], stand witness to how well Wolf succeeded and to the significance of her first major book. Christa Wolf continued to confound GDR critics and party officials with her next novel, *Nachdenken über Christa T.* [4]. They were especially dissatisfied with her "complex style", which stood in stark contrast to their demand for simplicity and in which they recognized — at least to some extent — the author's attempt to disguise in order to preempt and prevent a vetoing of publication. Not surprisingly, the book has a drawn-out editorial history before it was finally published in an extremely small edition.

The attempt to write in such a way that prose could be open to a wide range of interpretation — i.e., that critics positively inclined to what authors tried to accomplish would have the opportunity to reconcile these works with the official demands by offering acceptable interpretations — continued throughout the 1970's An excellent example is Ulrich Plenzdorf's *Die neuen Leiden des jungen W.* [5], in which the author tried to satisfy the dual demands of state mandates and of his

---

[1] Christa Wolf, *Des geteilte Himmel* (Munich: DTV, 1973).

[2] See Dieter Sevin, «The Plea for Artistic Freedom in Christa Wolf's *Lesen und Schreiben* and *Nachdenken über Christa T.*: Essay and Fiction as Mutually Supportive Genre Forms», in *Studies in GDR Culture and Society*, 2 (Washington D.C.: University Press of America, 1982), pp. 45-58.

[3] *Der geteilte Himmel und seine Kritiker. Dokumentation*, ed. by Martin Reso (Halle: Mitteldeutscher, 1965).

[4] Christa Wolf, *Nachdenken über Christa T.* (Darmstadt/Neuwied: Luchterhand, 1971).

[5] Ulrich Plenzdorf, *Die neue Leiden des jungen W.* (Frankfurt/M: Suhrkamp, 1976).

own personal, often conflicting convictions and concerns [6]. It is this process which contributed, in our opinion, to the enormous creativity and productivity of East German writers, and led to a high literary niveau, as recognized more and more beyond the geopolitical borders of the GDR.

With each successful publication of a controversial piece of literature, the limits of official tolerance seem to have been expanded to some extent. Experimentation appears to have been encouraged in the process, as authors could never be sure how far they could go nor where precisely the limits of acceptability might be at any one time. Even authors with a national and international reputation sometimes experienced that they had gone too far, such as Volker Braun with his *Unvollendete Geschichte* [7] which was published in the journal *Sinn und Form* (1975) but not as a book in the GDR. One aspect which probably aroused the censor's fury was Braun's candid exposure of the incompetency of leading officials as well as the ossification of state bureaucracy, culminating in a dream of a female factory worker which made clear that a renewal had to come and that it could come only from the disenfranchized working class.

During the last decade, until very recently, GDR authors continued to walk a tightrope between their desire to communicate and express to their readers what really concerned them and the fear of not being published at all in their own country. The topic of the arms' race and the urgent need to search for new ways to assure peace in an ever more dangerous world is a good example to illustrate our thesis. While the acellerating arms' race led to the formation of a mass peace movement in the West, official GDR policy did not permit any deviation from the official line that the new German Socialist state is a peace movement in itself, making superfluous any autonomous, independent movement by its citizens. The old line, that peace can be assured only through

---

[6] See Dieter Sevin, «The Reception of *Werther* in Ulrich Plenzdorf's *The New Suffering of Young W.*: Parody or Reincarnation of Goethe's Classic?» in *Goethe in the Twentieth Century,* ed. by Alexej Ugrinski (New York: Greenwood Press, 1987), pp. 67-76.

[7] Volker Braun, *Unvollendete Geschichte* (Frankfurt/M: Suhrkamp, 1979).

strength, also continued to be disseminated by the official media.

As often before in GDR literary history, when a topic could not officially be articulated or discussed, it found its way into literature. As a matter of fact, literature assumed by default an additional role, i.e., filling a societal need that in the West normally is met by the media. Literature became an *Informationsträger*, a disseminator and discussant of cogent issues. Indeed, the most prominent and thought-provoking GDR authors have been and are raising and discussing issues — all within the structure of their creative works — which are of vital concern in the GDR, problems which are not satisfactorily dealt with in the official media, the arms race. As the official prescription for peace did not satisfy an increasing number of critically thinking people, a number of authors felt compelled to reflect on the issue in their works. As illustration, we selected three major authors and works: Stefan Heym's *Ahasver* (1981); Christa Wolf's *Kassandra* (1983), and Volker Braun's *Hinze-Kunze-Roman* (1985).

Within the context of Heym's carefully researched prose work on the legendary figure of the wandering Jew, the topic of war and peace was interwoven primarily and most pointedly in the last third of his novel, when Ahasver encounters Jesus and tries to persuade him to change this world, since His promised Kingdom had not come: «Kein Schwert, entgegen dem Wort des Propheten, wurde je umgeschmiedet zur Pflugschar, kein Spiess zur Sichel geformt; vielmehr nehmen sie die geheimen Kräfte im All und machen daraus himmelhohe Pilze aus Flamme und Rauch, in denen alles Lebendige zu Asche wird und zu einem Schatten an der Wand» [8] Heym, whose works have not been published in the GDR since the early 1970's, might well have hoped that *Ahasver* would be acceptable in the GDR, since it was ostensibly far removed from our time. Yet Heym was not able or willing to sufficiently cloak his sharp and pointed criticism of present day reality, especially in regard to the peace issue. He is too explicit when invoking not only the image of the emblem of «swords into plowshares» — widely worn by GDR church youth and finally forbidden by the authorities — but also the Socialist emblem

---

[8] Stefan Heym, *Ahasver* (Munich: Bertelsmann, 1981), p. 211.

of the «sickle». Nor is he limiting his criticism with respect to the dangers of impending nuclear war one-sidedly toward the West which becomes quite apparent toward the end of the novel, where Ahasver reports about the second coming of Christ and his prophecies concerning Armageddon, the last battle of the world. There he vividly describes the resulting total destruction, emphasizing the bitterness of Reb Joshua — as Christ is called in the book — concerning the present condition of the world and the simple-mindedness of the men in charge of those horribly destructive arsenals: «Und von solchen Raketen ... gäbe es bereits viele Tausende, und diese ganze höllische Macht befinde sich in den Händen einiger weniger Herrscher, Männern mit beschränkter Denkungsart, die bei jeder Gelegenheit lauthals proklamierten, sie bräuchten ihr Arsenal zur Verteidigung des Friedens, denn der Frieden erfordere ein Gleichgewicht des Schreckens...» (Ahasver, 280). In this powerful prose the author obviously does not simply place the blame for the frightening situation solely on one side, but openly portrays his innermost fears and is pleading for sanity and change. The time, however, was not right for this kind of undisguised candidness and forceful formulation, and the novel was published only in the West, again without official permission.

Wolf's *Kassandra* [9] initially also appeared only in the Federal Republic — yet, in contrast to Heym, with official permission. In a very short time, *Kassandra* became an enormous success, the sole GDR novel on the best-seller list for almost a year. Several GDR editions followed shortly and were sold out quickly. How are we to explain the fact that Wolf's novel could be published — even though with difficulties — and not Heym's? After all, Wolf also does not hesitate to address the tough questions facing her society. While Wolf might be looked upon slightly more favorably by the ministry of culture because of her reputation, both authors are well-known and respected beyond the geopolitical borders of the GDR. The real reasons must therefore be sought in the works themselves, their style, structure and language.

Although the subject of both novels seem — at least on

---

[9] Christa Wolf, *Kassandra* (Darmstadt/Neuwied: Luchterhand, 1983).

the surface — far removed from present-day GDR reality, dating back to mythology and antiquity, the deeper meaning of both works reaches intensely into our times. The major difference is that Wolf's writing is much more subtle and less direct than Heym's and puts much greater demands on the reflexive processes of the reader. Wolf's prose work on the destruction of Troy and the ten years leading up to the final conquest by the Greeks is a parable of our endangered world. The author narrates the fictional account in the first person, from the perspective of Cassandra whose warnings were ignored, leading to the total destruction of a civilization. How and why could this have happened, is Cassandra's basic question. In the reader it inevitably raises the question if that could happen again in his own times and, if so, why?

While the first person narration, the analytical and questioning structure of the work stimulate the reflexive processes of the reader, Wolf adheres strictly to the historical frame throughout her novel, never relating events directly to present day reality. She does not need to, because certain issues — e.g. the unwillingness to negotiate, economic interests, the insane reliance on ever increasing armaments, false concepts of honor, and the fear of losing face — have not changed in three-thousand years. Other aspects are more difficult to understand and might not become clear to a reader, unless he is familiar with Wolf's «Frankfurt Poetic Lectures» [10] which deal primarily with her novel *Kassandra*. Such is the case with the possible allegorical meaning of Helena as a non-existent casus belli. In her Poetic Lectures, Wolf cites the dangers of using the revered words of «freedom» on one side and «socialism» on the other going to have the function Helena had during the Tojan War? Another question posed by the novel might be the modern parallel to the Trojan horse. In her Poetic Lectures, Wolf warns against modern industrialism which all societies seem to embrace as a panacea for all problems, but which might well carry the seeds of self-destruction within itself. Those critical passages, providing a possible answer as to what might bring about the ultimate destruction of civilization, are not accessible to the GRD reader, because the

---

[10] Christa Wolf, *Voraussetzungen einer Erzählung: Kassandra* (Darmstadt/Neuwied: Luchterhand, 1983).

Poetic Lectures were censored, when finally published in the GDR. Such cuts stand witness to the fact that even the most esteemed GDR authors are very much subject to the controls of the ministry of culture. It seems clear, therefore, that Wolf's Poetic Lectures were indeed intended solely for a Western audience. The open, candid, and indifferentiated criticism of issues like the arms' race could not have passed censorship. Furthermore, these lectures stand in stark contrast to the careful avoidance of formulations which could have placed the GDR publication of her novel in jeopardy. This awareness of the danger of non-publication — whether conscious or unconscious — was not detrimental. In fact, it seems to have contributed to the quality and fascination of this book, as it challenges the reader's reflexive processes to draw his own conclusions.

The thesis of this paper, namely that censorship can also have the paradoxical effect of stimulating the creative genius, seems to be supported even more by one of the most innovative and avantgarde of recent GDR novels, Volker Braun's *Hinze-Kunze-Roman* (1985). In a non-continuous string of episodes, a sheer firework of implications, satire and irony, the reader is constantly challenged to decide on the meaning of this text, which is stretching and expanding the limits of what had been acceptable by the authorities so far. Not surprisingly, it took four years before the book could finally be published in the GDR. The publisher, however, found it necessary to include an essay by the renowned GDR literary critic Dieter Schlenstedt in the appendix of the GDR edition, which must be seen as attempted justification and a guide for the «correct» reading of the work. Indeed, an unusual feature for a literary work and a strong indication about the uneasiness fo the editors concerning its publication, Schlenstedt emphasizes the *offene Sinnzentrum* (the open center of meaning) of Braun's work, which allows it to discuss and challenge the social reality of the GDR in a humorous, satirical, and sometimes grotesque manner.

The indebtedness to Diderot's *Jacques le Fataliste et Son Maitre* as well as to Goethe's *Faust* is undeniable, as Braun lets his protagonists Hinze and Kunze ride through the GDR in a black Russian limousine. The topic of war and peace represents in some ways the culmination of the problematic question about what is «in the social interest», a question posed almost like a *Leitmotif* throughout the text. In this discussion, Hinze — taking the role of Mephistopheles — tries to provoke his boss Kunze with a sarcastical thesis: «Man muss den Frieden weltweit herbeirüsten, dann wird er endgültig sein. Schliesslich ruft jeder Kernwaffentest... Veränderungen in der Gensubstanz hervor, die nicht reparabel sind. Der friedenssichernde Eifer muss unauslöschliche Erfolge zeitigen»[11]. The fact that such cynical pronouncements — and this is only one of many — could be published in the GDR, albeit with major difficulties, must be considered a major break-through in the trend toward liberalization in GDR literary affairs.

Whether Braun's work marks a turning point that will permanently alter the role and impact of GDR censorship, remains to be seen. Certainly there are indications of authors openly speaking up against the evils of censorship. Christoph Hein assaulted the existing practice most boldly at the Tenth GDR Writers' Congress in 1987, where he called censorship useless, outdated, paradoxical, inhumane, unconstitutional, and even criminal, and demanded that «die Zensur muss schnellstens und ersatzlos verschwinden, um weiteren Schaden von unserer Kultur abzuwenden»[12]. As of now, there are indications that Hein's words represent a real change, that Perestroika and Glasnost are indeed taking hold in the GDR. For instance, less than a year after the Tenth Writers' Congress, Volker Braun's *Unvollendete Geschichte* was finally published in the GDR, after a thirteen-year waiting period. Does that mean that GDR censorship is on the way out? And, if so, what effect would that have on a new generation of GDR writers? I suspect that, unless the changes are really dramatic, authors will continue to feel uncertain for some time. They will continue to walk the tightrope, to experiment, test, and expand permissible limits; and the literary genius will continue to flourish.

Dieter Sevin
Vanderbilt University

[11] Volker Braun, *Hinze-Kunze-Roman* (Halle/Leipzig: Mitteldeutscher, 1985), p. 199.

[12] Christoph Hein, «Literatur und Wirkung», in *X. Schriftstellerkongress der DDR* (Berlin/Weimar, Aufbau, 1988), p. 231.

LA COMMUNICATION DANS *UNE CHAINE DANS LE PARC* D'ANDRÉ LANGEVIN

André Langevin demeure pour plusieurs l'auteur d'un seul roman, publié en 1953: *Poussière sur la ville*. Les romans *Evadé de la nuit*, *Le temps des hommes*, *L'élan d'Amérique* ont reçu bien moins d'attention critique. En 1974 André Langevin publia *Une chaîne dans le parc*. Ce roman fut accueilli avec une indifférence peut-être plus grande encore, indifférence qu'il ne méritait certainement pas. Depuis, c'est le silence. André Langevin se tait. Or, c'est précisément ce dernier roman qui nous a frappée tant par sa qualité intensément poétique, que par le désir profond de créer un espace littéraire où la communication soit possible. Dans notre étude, nous nous proposons d'examiner un aspect important de l'itinéraire effectué vers cet espace dans le roman même, notamment le mouvement vers la parole quotidienne, linéaire abolie à travers la voix, le regard, les gestes et le toucher — moyens de communication qui n'ont point recours à la parole.

Pour introduire notre sujet, nous étudierons le passage-clef où Pierrot, personnage central du roman, raconte à Jane, son amie, son rêve de communication parfaite.

Les deux enfants Jane et Pierrot «s'en [vont] pour toujours» (*Ch*, 231) [1], «faire le tour du monde» (*Ch*, 233) et arrivent à «la banquise», «des pays qui flottent sur la mer du Pôle Nord» (*Ch*, 232). Les enfants descendent dans ce pays qui est creux. Il s'agit donc d'un grand voyage sur mer, et d'un mouvement de descente. Ce mouvement de descente peut être perçu comme un mouvement vers le rêve, ou la quête

---

[1] André Langevin, *Une chaîne dans le parc*. Paris: Julliard, 1974. Dorénavant nous indiquerons le roman par le sigle *Ch*, suivi de la page à laquelle nous renvoyons dans l'édition ci-dessus.

d'une réalité autre que la réalité quotidienne. Dans ce pays de glace tout est vert. Le vert est à la fois condition de vie et signe de danger: «Il n'y a pas de vie sans vert» (*Ch, 234*) mais «quand l'ours devient vert, ça veut dire qu'il y a du danger» (*Ch, 232*). Endroit privilégié où la coexistence des contraires est possible. Le monde «vert» est un monde qui appartient aux enfants. C'est un pays où «il n'y a pas d'argent, pas de travail, pas d'école» et où «il n'y a pas de policiers non plus» alors que le monde des «grandes personnes» (*Ch, 234*) est un monde caractérisé par ces mêmes éléments. Puisqu'il y a une loi, dans ce monde des adultes, «monde du bien» [2], il faut aussi qu'il y ait des «policiers» (*Ch, 234*). Dans le monde merveilleux du pays vert, le temps est un éternel présent de bonheur et de liberté. «Je veux dire qu'ils deviennent jamais des grandes personnes [...] ils sont en enfants pendant cent ans, puis alors ils grandissent tout d'un coup en cinq minutes, et ils meurent» (*Ch, 234*) explique Pierrot. La mort survient comme un fait extérieur et non pas comme le résultat d'une lente destruction [3]. Et dans ce pays de l'enfance merveilleuse, pays qui s'oppose au monde quotidien, une parfaite communication des consciences est possible: «et personne ne parle, parce qu'ils ont tous le sens de lire dans la tête des autres» (*Ch, 234*). La communication ici est l'expérience immédiate d'autrui. Ce sens dont parle Pierrot remplace la parole et constitue une profonde intuition d'autrui. Le langage est aboli, car il ne fait que troubler cette transparence immédiatement donnée. Le «sens de lire dans la tête des autres» se rapporte au rêve de transparence et à l'espace marin où se situe le pays vert. La transparence symboliserait l'abolition de tout ce qui est murs, barrières ou opacité, éléments hostiles à la communication.

Nous relevons donc, dans le rêve des enfants verts, l'aspiration vers le silence (le rêve de la parole abolie), et vers la

---

[2] Voir G. Bataille, *L'érotisme*, Paris: éditions de Minuit, 1957.

Georges Bataille distingue entre le monde du «bien», des «lois» et du «travail» d'une part, et le monde «sacré» d'autre part. Ainsi: «Le travail a déterminé l'opposition du monde sacré et du monde profane» (*L'érotisme*, 126).

[3] Dans *La littérature et le mal*, Georges Bataille explique: «La divine ivresse à laquelle s'apparente le "mouvement primesautier" de l'enfance est en entier dans le présent» (Saint-Amand: Gallimard, 1957, p. 21).

transparence (le don de lire dans la tête d'autrui). L'espace-temps privilégié est celui du monde sacré, du monde de l'enfance, de l'eau et du rêve.

LE LANGAGE-OBSTACLE

Si Pierrot rêve à une communication où le langage serait aboli, c'est que souvent c'est ce langage même qui constitue le plus grand obstacle à toute véritable communication. Le langage-obstacle est fait de mots-objets, de mots pétrifiés et opaques. Ainsi, lorsque Pierrot se sent étranger à Jane, il observe: «Elle lui paraît étrangère, aussi hors de sa vie que les poteaux de bois ou le mot KIK écrit en grosses lettres» (*Ch*, 130). Le langage linéaire déforme la réalité tout en la figeant; Pierrot s'en rend compte en relisant son cahier: «les mots ont emprisonné des moments qui n'ont jamais été si nets, ni isolés, comme des phrases» (*Ch*, 112). Impossibilité de traduire le pour-soi du vécu en langage sans le chosifier. Devant l'obstacle insurmontable que constitue le langage, Pierrot se sent profondément découragé:

> Telle que racontée dans le cahier, l'histoire existe à peine, parce qu'il y a des trous si grands entre les jours, que ce qui s'est le plus passé ne s'y trouve pas, et que ce qu'on peut lire demanderait tellement d'explications qu'il serait plus simple de lire dans sa tête (*Ch*, 113).

Le langage linéaire échoue à rendre compte d'une dimension essentielle, celle de l'intensité du vécu, et rend impossible une communication véritable. Pierrot formule, une fois de plus, l'idéal d'une communication des consciences: «lire dans sa tête». D'ailleurs à la linéarité et à la chosification du langage s'ajoute sa pauvreté: face à la richesse infinie de la vie, les mots sont insuffisants et le langage est issentiellement pauvre. Lorsque l'oncle Napoleón donne un dollar à Pierrot et à Jane, Pierrot aimerait lui exprimer sa reconnaissance, mais les mots lui manquent: «il accouche d'un pitoyable —Bonjour et merci, mon oncle» (*Ch*, 170). Pitoyable en effet, car la petite phrase ne communique point. Pierrot vient à se méfier de ce langage traître. Lorsqu'il revoit Jane après une séparation, et qu'il en est tout heureux, il a peur de parler: les mots aux contours si raides risquent de faire disparaître tout le charme: «... de la retrouver ainsi [...] la rend si précieuse qu'un seul mot de lui va sûrement la faire éclater comme une bulle de savon» (*Ch.* 144).

Non seulement le langage linéaire devient-il dans le roman un véritable obstacle à la communication mais encore pour atteindre à la véritable communication, il s'agit d'aller au-delà de ce langage-obstacle, d'abolir la parole inerte, de créer ce silence privilégié où pourront naître une nouvelle communication, une parole poétique.

VERS LA PAROLE ABOLIE

La voix.—Alors que les mots constituent des obstacles à la communication, il y a d'autres modes de communication possibles, modes qui tendent à abolir progressivement la parole courante. Si l'en-soi est objet inerte, la désincarnation est une condition favorable à la communication. L'homme en bleu, personnage mystérieux et central dans le roman, apparaît aux enfants, pour la première fois, comme «une grande ombre» et comme «una belle voix profonde» (*Ch.* 182). La voix dans ce sens se trouve à mi-chemin entre le langage déjà aboli, et le silence: elle rejoint en ceci la musique. Lorsque Pierrot rencontre Gaston pour la première fois, leur contact est violent: les paroles aussi bien que les gestes. Pourtant, ce ne soit ni ces gestes, ni les paroles de Gaston qui font mal à Pierrot, car il sent que la véritable intention de Gaston n'est point de lui faire du mal. C'est la voix qui frappe Pierrot: «mais la voix sans souffle lui fait plus mal que les mains qui s'enfoncent dans sa chemise. Une voix frileuse, qui ne devrait pas sortir, même au soleil...» (*Ch.* 22). La voix raconte ce que les mots ne disent pas: une communication mystérieuse s'établit. Jane et Emily sont soeurs par la voix. C'est par leurs voix que l'on cerne leurs caractéristiques communes: «Les deux voix se ressemblent même dans leur façon de se percher haut pour se tenir à distance et exprimer tour le froid du monde [...]» (*Ch.* 213). Ainsi, on découvre autrui par l'intermédiaire de la voix. Il arrive aussi que la voix nous révèle à nous-mêmes. Pierrot bat tante Maria qui a essayé de détruire ce qu'il avait de plus précieux dans l'intimité de sa conscience. Il est hors de lui. «Et c'est sa propre voix qu'il n'a jamais entendue, qui crie: —Putain! Ivrogne! Bordel! Grosse cochonne!» (*Ch*, 255). A travers sa voix, Pierrot découvre en soi l'être de la transgression, l'être qui viole les interdits. Nous savons que la communication est avant tout ouverture; une telle ouverture peut s'effectuer par la voix: la voix de Gaston est «écorchée» (*Ch*, 24), dépouillée donc de son écorce, de toute protection ou barrière.

Alors que les mots restent souvent à la surface des choses, la voix pénètre autrui. Pour Pierrot, la voix de Jane est «la voix grave à reflets d'eau qui vibre dans ses veines» (*Ch*, 79). Un rapport en profondeur s'établit grâce à cette voix. Pierrot écoute Jane parler, mais c'est la voix qui le fascine:

> Il voudrait qu'elle continue de parler sans jamais s'arrêter, pas pour les mots, pour le son de sa voix seulement, pour cette musique qui ébranle tous ses nerfs [...] (*Ch*, 144).

Notons la progression dans le degré de communication atteint: tandis que dans le premier cas, c'était la voix de Jane qui vibrait dans les veines de Pierrot, dans le second la voix de Jane fait vibrer les nerfs de Pierrot. La voix d'Emily, comme celle de Jane, «remue les entrailles» (*Ch*, 212). Alors que la communication par les mots implique des processus mentaux tels la raison et l'intellect, la voix communique d'une façon immédiate. Notons les limites de la voix, ses paroxysmes; le rire, comme d'ailleurs le sanglot, est convulsif. Ainsi que les autres manifestations de la voix, le rire établit une communication immédiate. Jane rit: «L'eau profonde de son rire, ainsi qu'une main fraîche sur sa poitrine brûlante» (*Ch*, 144). Image fascinante où s'opère une synesthésie entre l'ouïe, le goût et le toucher. Le rire désaltère, le rire est l'eau. Or, dit Bachelard: «[...] d'abord tout liquide est une eau; ensuite toute eau est un lait» [4]. En effet, le son de la voix de Jane est comparé au lait: «le son de sa voix dans sa propre poitrine, un lait doux et chaud» (*Ch*, 83). Lait chaud, la voix est intériorisée par autrui comme élément nécessaire à sa survie.

---

[4] Gaston Bachelard, *L'eau et le rêves*, Paris: Corti, 1942, p. 158.

La voix transmet la tristesse ou le contentement. Lorsqu'elle vient de pleurer, Jane parle «d'une voix plus mouillée que l'eau» (*Ch*, 214). Heureuse ou triste donc, la voix qui communique est une eau, un liquide, une continuité qui coule. D'autre part la voix qui refuse de communiquer devient discontinue. Isabelle s'adressant à Paul (qu'elle n'aime pas) parle «d'une voix pleine de trous» (*Ch*, 207). Mais alors que les mots peuvent mentir, la voix ne ment point. Toute divergence entre l'intention et le son éclate. Si comme nous venons de le voir, le rire sincère établit une communication immédiate, le rire qui est du «théâtre» est reconnu tout de suite comme faux. «Jane éclate de rire, mais son rire se prolonge en une sorte de gloussement qui sonne faux, comme si quelqu'un d'autre l'entendait» (*Ch*, 182). De même, le rire du Rat est toujours associé à des dissonances: «[il] souffle un rire qui n'en finit pas de grincer dans sa gorge» (*Ch*, 152). C'est que face à la mort, le rire franc, ouvert, est impossible. Alors que les mots peuvent masquer la pensée, la voix artificielle trahit celui qui l'utilise, dénonçant le déguisement. Pierrot «s'efforc[e] de prendre lui aussi, une voix heureuse, mais elle chevrote comme celle de Maria [...]» (*Ch*, 272) et Jane, parlant de Gaston, prend «un air de grande dame» (*Ch*, 166) et par conséquent parle «d'une voix à talons hauts» (*Ch*, 166). Sa voix haut perchée, aiguë est prétentieuse. C'est parce que la voix dit vrai, que, avant de se suicider, l'homme en bleu parle d'une voix qui est détachée de lui «une voix [...] qui parle toute seule» (*Ch*, 285-286).

Le regard.—Les mots ainsi que la voix provoquent l'attention, mais le regard la suppose déjà: le regard implique une prédisposition à la communication. Tandis que le chat Balibou se métamorphoses sans cesse et devient tour à tour serpent et cheval, ses yeux verts restent toujours les mêmes. C'est que les yeux expriment l'essence intime de l'être, essence indépendante des apparences. Peut-être, grâce à ceci, le regard réussit-il là où les mots échouent: Jane se refuse à attribuer un sens aux mots de la chanson anglaise que chante Gaston. Mais elle ne peut rejeter aussi facilement la fascination qu'exerce sur elle le regard du Rat. Lorsque (après avoir entendu la chanson) elle peut finalement partir, elle se jette dans les bras de Pierrot: «Jane est déjà dans ses bras, un peu tremblante, un peu secouée par les mots, mais libérée surtout du regard affamé du Rat» (*Ch*, 163). Il y a des messages qui ne se transmettent que par le regard: le Rat a reçu sa guitare et il en est heureux. Son bonheur s'exprimera non pas par des paroles, mais par son corps et surtout par son regard: «Le Rat [...] est heureux et le laisse voir [...] dans le rire vert de son regard» (*Ch*, 157). Notons ici la couleur verte que nous avons relevée pour le pays rêvé de la communication parfaite, ainsi que le phénomène de la synesthésie; le regard est couleur et voix à la fois. D'ailleurs non pas une voix quelconque, mais une voix du paroxysme (du rire). Lorsque Jane est déçue de voir l'homme en bleu avec sa soeur, elle l'exprime par les mots aussi bien que par le regard: «Elle se dresse sur ses pieds à lui pour être à la hauteur et exprimer par son regard plus que par les mots, l'indifférence agressive de l'amour trompé» (*Ch*, 213). Le regard révèle ce qu'il y a de plus secret dans l'âme et rend ainsi possible la communion des consciences. Pierrot découvre dans le regard de Jane «une lumière immobile, un deuxième être beaucoup plus grave, si en retrait [...] qu'elle ne connaît pas elle-même peut-être et avec qui on ne peut parler» (*Ch*, 202). Mais la communication est bilatérale. Le regard qui révèle sait aussi pénétrer et voir autri à travers les apparences parfois trompeuses. Pierrot sait qu'il aimerait Jane, même si elle devenait laide «parce qu'elle ne changera jamais dans sa tête» (*Ch*, 151). Nous retrouvons ici un élément du rêve des enfants verts. La capacité de voir dans la tête d'autrui est une capacité appartenant au domaine du regard. Telle la voix qui trahit l'interlocuteur lorsqu'il n'est pas sincère, le regard aussi trahit ce que la personne tâche de masquer. Tante Rose, malgré son «ton maussade habituel», a «un peu de gêne ou de honte dans les yeux» (*Ch*, 217) lorsque Pierrot la surprend rangeant dans une boîte son costume de l'orphelinat (c'est qu'elle a l'intention, avec l'oncle de renvoyer Pierrot). Lorsque Papapouf est triste et soucieux, ses yeux démentent la gaieté de ses propos.

Les gestes.—Comme le regard, le geste présuppose l'attention et donc une disponibilité à la communication. Comme la voix et le regard, les gestes constituent un langage. Le geste est avant tout mouvement: il vit et communique. Lorsque Sainte Agnès touche le front de Pierrot malade, c'est ce geste unique qui traduit toute l'amitié que Sainte Agnès éprouve pour l'enfant. Il ne s'agit pas du toucher, Pierrot rend cela bien clair: «et quand elle a touché mon front, je n'ai rien senti» (*Ch*, 114). C'est le geste, le mouvement et l'intention qui lui a donné naissance, qui crée le miracle de la communication:

> la révélation tout à coup [d'une présence...] [...] Une communication semblable à celles dont il n'osait pas s'avouer à lui-même la faim dans ses rêves les moins avouables, et par un geste vivant de femme (*Ch*, 114).

Le simple geste établit donc une communication rêvée, parfaite. En fait, le plus simple des gestes peut créer des liens. Lorsque, par exemple, Jane suit Pierrot

> [...] quand il se retourne, elle est immobile sur l'autre palier, une jambe en l'air, et un doigt sur la bouche pour lui indiquer de se taire. Ce simple geste de complicité le comble de joie (*Ch*, 62).

C'est que Pierrot reconnaît l'importance d'un geste. A l'orphelinat, «dans le silence des murs», pendant de longues périodes, il ne communiquait «que par signes» (*Ch*, 62). Le geste a donc pu triompher du silence, car il avait une signification, il était signe.

Le toucher.—Il y a trois phases à toute communication véritable: l'être isolé qui comme le dit Blanchot: «doit être brisé pour devenir lui-même» [5]; l'être perdu à soi (l'être du silence et de la mort); l'être retrouvé à soi dans son rapport avec autrui (communication). Cet itinéraire menant à la communication peut être facilement retracé dans l'histoire du baiser échangé par Jane et Pierrot par-dessus le vide. C'est aussi bien l'histoire d'une communication parfaite établie au moyen du toucher. La première phase est celle de l'individu isolé: Pierrot et Jane se trouvent l'un face à l'autre sur deux balcons voisins séparés par un vide. La distance (le vide dans

---

[5] Maurice Blanchot, *Le livre à venir* (Saint-Amand: éditions Gallimard, 1959), p. 102.

76

ce cas) paraît insurmontable. Dans le roman le vide représente au niveau symbolique un obstacle à la communication (rappelons par exemple la voix «pleine de trous» d'Isabelle). Ici le figuré et le littéral se rejoignent. Il faut nous rappeler à présent que la communication comporte une dimension de risque: la couleur verte du pays des enfants verts, n'est-elle pas le symbole de la vie aussi bien que du danger de mort? Jane ne considère pas le vide comme infranchissable; elle passe pardessus la balustrade de fer:

> Les talons appuyés au rebord, les deux mains tendues dans son dos, tenant l'appui, et tout le corps arqué dans le vide, oiseau blanc et roux, et follement amusé, elle s'apprête à prendre son vol (*Ch*. 145).

L'oiseau est «follement amusé»! Evidemment, car c'est un oiseau. Mais l'enfant Jane, l'enfant si humain et qui ne sait point voler, s'amuse bien follement et prend des risques fous. Pierrot suit l'exemple de Jane; à son tour, il se tient au-dessus du vide. Pierrot et Jane se perdent à soi, ils perdent leur être social et risquent absolument tout. Le vide est surmonté: Jane «donne un violent coup de tête et la mousse rousse le caresse et l'aveugle» (*Ch*, 145). La caresse, premier contact et signe de tendresse, aveugle. Pour acquérir une vision privilégiée (poétique), il faut passer par l'aveuglement, tout comme pour acquérir le verbe poétique il faut passer par le silence. Pierrot et Jane se trouvent dans un espace-temps sacré (au-dessus du vide), ils ont quitté le temps profane en transgressant ses lois (en risquant leur vie). La société, la rue, les regarde d'en bas ahurie, sans comprendre. Car Jane et Pierrot n'agissent pas selon les règles de l'intérêt; ils risquent leur vie, ils renversent l'ordre du monde. C'est précisément pour cela que Pierrot regardant vers le bas, vers la rue, «voit le monde à l'envers» (*Ch*, 145). Les enfants risquent tout (leur vie), et ils gagnent tout. Vient le baiser au «goût fulgurant» (*Ch*, 146). Notons en passant une synesthésie de plus, celle du goût et de la vision. La communication parfaite est extrêmement vive, intense, mais aussi de très courte durée comme l'indique le terme «fulgurant». C'est ce moment qui donne à Pierrot «le vertige» (*Ch*, 146). Le renversement opéré est complet: les enfants se trouvent au-dessus d'un vide bien réel, les risque est énorme, mais le vide ne provoque aucun vertige. C'est le baiser, le contact qui crée le vertige. C'est l'espace intérieur entré en un contact unique avec l'extérieur qui donne le vertige. C'est cet espace concentré que Blanchot appelle «pur moment essentiel, [...]goutte de lumière»[6] et que Pierrot nomme «moment fulgurant».

Abondent dans le roman d'autres moments où une communication profonde s'établi grâce au toucher: ces moments racontent la possibilité d'un contact-toucher très naturel, donnant par là l'impression de facilité. Jane, sortant toute mouillée du bassin d'eau, embrasse Pierrot: «Elle a fait si vite que ce n'est que longtemps après qu'il frissonne sous l'eau fraîche de ses lèvres» (*Ch*, 80). Le toucher est ici une eau fraîche, un liquide régénérateur. Cette eau se transforme forcément en lait. Maman Pouf embrasse Pierrot: «Elle l'embrasse, comme elle donne le sein, sans y penser, parce que la paix lui coule de partout et qu'elle doit en nourrir les autres» (*Ch*, 262). La paix c'est le lait maternel, et le contact avec maman Pouf nourrit et donne vie. Thérèse embrasse sa mère et son petit frère: «Elle embrasse à la fois l'enfant et le sein et tout le soleil du jardin frémit dans le lait de maman Pouf [...]» (*Ch*, 92). Pour maman Pouf ainsi que pour Thérèse, établir le contact à travers le toucher (embrasser autrui) est la chose la plus naturelle au monde. Ce rapport est entièrement immédiat, irréfléchi, presque animal. Maman Pouf embrasse «sans y penser», ou encore «maman Pouf parvient facilement à les étreindre tous les deux d'un seul bras, et elle les lèches comme une chatte» (*Ch*, 208). Le toucher n'est superficiel qu'en apparence. En fait, toucher signifie souvent pénétrer d'une manière très profonde, atteindre à l'essence. Jane pleure, mais Pierrot, par pudeur, ne touche pas à sa joue: «pour savoir si elle a pleuré, il lui faudrait toucher sa joue, mais ce serait comme mettre les doigts dans son coeur» (*Ch*, 214). Lorsque Jane et Pierrot passent la nuit dans la maison abandonnée, Pierrot «s'endort tout doucement, sa main recueillant un à un les petits battements de coeur si chauds de Jane» (*Ch*, 294). Le toucher communique ici la vie même.

---

[6] Idem, p. 96.

CONCLUSION

Nous avons examiné quelques moyens de communication qui se passaient bien de la parole, et qui menaient vers le silence. En analysant la voix, le regard, les gestes, le toucher, nous avons noté quelques synesthésies. Pourquoi ces associations de perception appartenant au domaine d'un sens avec une image appartenant au domaine d'un autre sens? Nous avons vu qu'une voix pouvait «remuer les entrailles» (*Ch*, 212), de même qu'on pouvait se noyer dans les yeux d'autrui: «[Pierrot] se noie dans l'eau sombre de ses yeux» (*Ch,* 61). Enfin les cheveux de Jane sont l'eau et le soleil: «une fontaine de soleil roux» (*Ch,* 64). Georges Bataille commente sur cette sorte de synesthésie:

> La poésie mène au même point que l'indistinction, à la confusion des objets distincts. Elle nous mène à la mort, et par la mort, à la continuité [7].

Il est bien évident que dans l'espace sacré du silence qui survient après l'abolition du langage linéaire, un verbe poétique peut naître. C'est précisément grâce à un tel verbe qu'*Une chaîne dans le parc* est un si beau roman.

Irene Oore
Dalhousie University

---

[7] G. Bataille, *L'érotisme* (Paris: Editions de Minuit, 1957), p. 30.

CONTEMPTUS VITAE AULICAE ET LAUS RURIS (UTOPIAN CONCEPTS OF COUNTRY LIFE IN GERMAN BAROQUE NOVELS)

With this paper's Latin title which of course is borrowed from Aegidius Albertinus I want to indicate the line of argument I intend to pursue: I shall trace the topic of country life in some German novels of the 17th century and hope to show that their authors never intended to give a realistic portrayal of rural life in their times. Rather, these descriptions represent utopian concepts that describe an ideal locality or situation. German novelists of the 17th century were not after the verisimilitude we find in the 19th century realist. When baroque writers describe nature and country life they express that longing which usually befalls societies when a certain state of civilization has been achieved and the direct contact with nature has been lost. In western literature this theme has a long tradition. Well known early examples are Horace's *Epodes* and Virgil's *Georgica,* and since we will be discussing novels it should not be forgotten that the pastoral *Daphnis and Chloe* (3rd century A.D.) is one of the prototypes of the genre in antiquity.

There is no time today to pursue the history of the pastoral theme through the ages. Instead I would like to take you with a giant leap into the 16th century. This era marked the transition from feudalism to absolutism and produced several theoretical works on political theory, the most prominent of which is Niccolo Machiavelli's *Il Principe* (1532). While courtly life flourished in the 16th and 17th centuries, there was also opposition to a life style which was seen by many as unnatural and indeed immoral. To this day Machiavelli has lent his name to the characterization of immoral —not amoral as he meant it — politics. One of the literary responses to the artificiality of court and city life was a renewed interest in a supposedly innocent and simple existence in the country. The anti-court sentiment of fiction writers usually took the form of satire or of an idealistic portrayal of the pleasures of rural life. This I see as one of the reasons for the resurgence of bucolic literature in 16th century Europe.

While many of the west European literary trends reached Germany rather late in the 17th century we can establish with great accuracy the entry point for the resurgence of the idea that rural life is morally superior. After the Ecumenical Council of Trent had approved the use of literature as a weapon of the Counter-Reformation there was an influx into Germany of west European writings on moral theology. Perhaps the most influential writer in this field was the Spaniard Antonio de Guevara (1480-1545) whose works were translated and popularized by Aegidius Albertinus (1560-1620), secretary to the dukes of Bavaria. His German translation of Guevara's *Menosprecio de corte y alabanza de aldea* appeared in 1598 under the Latin title «Contemptus vitae aulica et laus ruris» [1]. This small treatise became extremely popular and over a span of a hundred years saw many editions and reprints. It formulates a theme which was to run through German literature for several centuries.

After this lengthy introduction to a brief paper, I shall now concentrate on the novel. To avoid misunderstanding I would like to state that I see bucolic or pastoral literature in the 17th centry just as *one* form of what Klaus Garber calls «Landlebendichtung», literature of country life [2]. It can have a much wider scope than bucolic literature [3]. Johann Beer's novels which I will discuss later are a case in point. They represent much more than a mere outcropping of pastoral

---

[1] Aegidius Albertinus, *Zwey schöne Tractätl / dern das eine Contemptus Vitae Aulicae & Laus Ruris: intitulirt* [...] *Das ander aber: De conviviis & compotationibus* [...], München, 1598.

[2] Klaus Garber, *Der Locus amoenus und der Locus terribilis*, Köln, 1974.

[3] Anke Lohmeir, «Zur Bestimmung der deutschen Landlebendichtung», *Schäferdichtung*, edit. Wilhelm Vopkamp, Hamburg, 1977, 123-140, esp. 125: «Der Gattung "Landlebendichtung" möchte ich einen Text jedoch nur dann zuordnen, wenn die "laus ruris" diesen Text ausfüllt, d.h. also als übergeordnetes, zentrales Thema einer geschlossenen literarischen Form fungiert».

literature. Rather, they are reflecting a general mood of which one possible manifestation is the pastoral novel. Without going into any detail I will take a brief look at the latter by reminding you of the archetypical scene of the pastoral novel in Zesens *Adriatische Rosemund* (1645) in which the heroine has withdrawn to a life in rural surroundings outside of Amsterdam. Although Garber sees indications that Zesen as the only 17th century writer is anticipating a new attitude towards nature which was not to become popular until much later, the situation reflects *an idealized concept* of a shepherdess's life. It has very little to do with reality but owes to the traditional topos [4].

Another example of the idealization of country life is Johann Joseph Beckh's *Elbianische Florabella* (1667) [5]. Although some of Beckh's nature descriptions in this pastoral novel show elements of realism he also clearly follows a traditional literary topos when he uses the shepherd's milieu [6]. It must also be remembered that a «realistic» nature description does not necessarily represent «Landleben». For this, human interaction with the rural environment is needed. As is the case in similar novels Beckh's shepherds are a group of friends who share a common interest in poetry, music and dance. In keeping with tradition they gather on a pleasant meadow under a linden tree. Their sheep are mere ciphers that are not even worthy of the author's description. How freely pastoral writers play with the elements of country life is illustrated by recent biographic research. It shows that the sheep owned by Beckh's autobiographical protagonist reflect the number of guilders the author had inherited. That this type of pastoral literature with its animals and «loci amoeni» was just a manifestation of the traditional topos, and not an attempt to represent true country life, becomes evident when we remember to what extent «Schäferwesen» soon became just another form of courtly entertainment in the 17th and 18th centuries, thereby loosing the last vestige of its claim to be a foil to court life. For an illustration you just have to look at some rococo paintings.

---

[4] Garber, 162 f.
[5] Johann Joseff Bekkhs/gekröhnten Poetens *Elbianische Florabella* [...], Dresden, 1667.
[6] Garber, 164 f.

Well then, what about writers who have been acclaimed
for their realism? When they portray country life are they as
well merely conjuring up a utopia or do they depict life as
they could see it all around them. If we take a look at the
opening chapters of Grimmelshausen's *Simplicissimus* it is
easy to see that no realistic description of rural existence is
intended [7]. Firstly, there is the ironical mode of the narrative,
and secondly, Grimmelshausen's intention of projecting the
natural state of humanity before the Fall is quite evident. It
is the utopia of the «Golden Age» he is aiming at as a foil for
the cruel and very real world he is about to describe. The
Jupiter episode and even more the protagonist's encounter
with the sylph society in the Mummelsee chapters demonstrate
clearly that utopian concepts play an important role in *Simplicissimus*. This confirms my interpretation of the rural scene
at the beginning of the novel as an imaginary concept rather
than a mimetic description. Since there is only a limited time
allotment, I have to restrict my remarks on Grimmelshausen
to this cursory and superficial comment on his major work.
With regard to his lesser novels a shift in emphasis towards
a greater interest in actual country life could probably be
argued.

So far we have looked at texts which in my opinion do
not have the depiction of rural life as their major objective.
I will now move on to Johann Beer who in two pieces that are
usually called his Willenhag novels used country life as background for his plot [8]. Indeed many would argue that country
life *is* the main topic of *Die teutschen Winter-Nächte* and *Die
Kurtzweiligen Sommertäge*. The two novels correspond more
closely to Anke Lohmeier's definition of «Landlebendichtung»
than any other 17th century novel I know [9]. They describe a
happy life in the country that is almost independent of events
taking place outside the scope of the novel, in the *real* world.
Both novels, one of which is a slightly disguised continuation

---

[7] With regard to Grimmelshausen's realism and his portrayal of
country life, see: Hans Dieter Gebauer, *Grimmelshausens Bauerndar-
stellung*, Marburg, 1977, esp. 251 f.; and R. P. T. Aylett, *The Nature
of Realism in Grimmelshausen's Simplicissimus Cycle of Novels*,
Bern 1982.

[8] Johann Beer, *Die teutschen Winter-Nächte & Die Kurzweiligen
Sommer-Täge*, Frankfurt, 1963.

[9] L. c.

of the other, formalistically represent a mixture of the types of novels that dominated German 17th century prose, something that for want of a better term has been called a «Mischform». They show a strong influence of the picaresque novel, but also elements of the pastoral and the courtly-historical novels. What makes Beer's novels unique and is totally new in the category of quasirealistic novel is the stratum of society that furnished the cast of characters. While the protagonists of other Baroque novels are either the rogues of the picaresque novel, the high nobility of the courtly novel or the middle class people usually found in German pastoral novels, Beer chooses the landed gentry, the «Landadel». Against a landscape which Alewyn and other researchers have identified as that of the author's original home in the lake district of Upper Austria, Beer describes the lives, loves and frolics of a group of friends that occupy adjacent estates [10]. Many of the details of running an estate that are mentioned in passing seem to reflect reality. Examples like these and similar detailed descriptions in Beer's novel *Jucundus Jucundissimus* [11] furnished the evidence for Alewyn's somewhat overstated claim for Beer's realism that he saw as far superior to Grimmelshausen's «naturalism» [12]. However, the narrative is strangely devoid of any historical reference point, with the exception of some allusions to the peasants' war that had raged in this part of Austria some fifty years before Beer wrote the novels and of which he could only know from hearsay. The frequent use of place-names of Upper Austria, and those that are invented but which sound Austrian, evokes a certain type of landscape. Yet something appears to be lacking to make it real. The answer seems to be that Beer is able to evoke the image of a landscape by using all the right elements in order to work on the readers' imagination. The fact that this landscape is brought back from memory and therefore also imagined by the creator of the text makes the transfer to the recipient even more effective. Jörg-Jochen Müller whose study on the Willenhag novels is the most comprehensive characterizes

---

[10] Alewyn, 116.

[11] Johann Beer, *Das Narrenspital sowie Jucundi Jucundissimi Wunderliche Lebens-Beschreibung*, Hamburg, 1957.

[12] Alewyn, 196-225; Gebauer, 251-259, criticizes Alewyn's theory. Also see Jörg-Jochen Müchen, Marburg, 1965, 106-112.

Beer's time and place references as deliberately avoiding any connection to the nonfictional world. Regarding the geographical information provided in the novels, Müller writes that through a mixture of actual and fictional place names a new *literary* landscape is created [13]. Alewyn, in a way, also acknowledged this situation by demonstrating that the effect of landscape on Beer's imagination is inversely proportional to their geographical and temporal proximity to the author [14]. The people who populate the novel are similarly real and unreal at the same time. The main preoccupation of the protagonists, who are hardly ever bothered by concerns for their economic situation, seems to be to celebrate weddings, baptisms and to enjoy lavish feasts. To add to this kind of entertainment they play a never ending string of pranks on each other, ride out, hunt or go on sleigh rides. When things really threaten to become dull they listen to the life story of some vagrant who conveniently drops in at the right moment. It would appear therefore that Beer was not describing what he saw or had seen and remembered but rather an imagined world that he would have found desirable. Beer published the two novels while living with a wife and a growing number of children in Weifenfels where he was a court musician, which leads me to conclude that he used his prolific imagination to conjure up a literary portrayal of a fictitious life which was a foil or his real life. As we know from his biography and his own diary. Beer had hardly any contact with members of the lower nobility living on their estates in the countryside [15]. Instead he was well received at the court where he rubbed shoulders with the high nobility and was appreciated as a humorous entertainer at the Duke's table. Apart from his duties at the court his private life was somewhat dull. As far as we know he never again saw his native Austria which he had left at age fifteen. There is also no indication to confirm Alewyn's speculation that Beer had ever lived on a country estate before leaving Austria.

My conclusion then is this: Beer in his most highly regar-

---

[13] Müller, 262-266.

[14] Alewyn, 117.

[15] For a reliable recent biography see: James Hardin *Johann Beer*, Boston, 1980; Johann Ber, *Sein Leben, von ihm selbst erzählt,* edit. Adolf Schmiedeke, Göttingen, 1965.

ded novels is developing his own private «Utopia» of a life free from everyday duties and obligations and struggles with competitors. In his fantasies he tried to escape the rather oppressive life of the petite bourgeoisie of which his diary draws such a drab picture. If, given a choice, he would have opted for the idyllic country life he described remains doubtful. He seems to have been quite content with the official side of his life as entertainer and confidant of his master the Duke. There, by his craft as a musician and by his wit he had managed to bridge the gap between his middle class background and the high nobility of the day. His allegedly realistic descriptions fall in the category of utopian visions of a Golden Age that either has been lost long ago or perhaps never existed.

A true portrayal of rural life independent of the traditional literary topos was hardly possible in the 17th century. Only the «Gefühlskultur» of the 18th century brought a true change in attitudes when the stylized fixation of nature is finally lifted. Only then could the depiction of country life in literature begin to represent more than a utopia.

Manfred K. Kremer
University of Guelph

THE WRITER'S APPRENTICESHIP: SPECULAR AND SPECULATIVE READING IN THE BUTORIAN TEXT

I don't think Butor would take offense at my use of the term «apprenticeship» as metaphor for his activity as writer. Despite an amply demonstrated mastery of the written word, Butor has even quite recently represented himself as «l'étudiant Michel Butor [qui] passait les nuits à combiner des plans, et les jours à modeler les longues phrases destinées à orner ces volumes»[1]. To be sure, the writer's implied selfsubordination to great writers (and to the «grand éditeur») has an unmistakably ironic edge to it, for it appears in the penultimate essay of the final volume of his vast *Répertoires*. The series' title as much as its content plays with the double notion of apprenticeship/mastery; his essays display a reader's rendition of the cultural masters, hence, demonstrate his mastery of a repertoire, as well as his writerly virtuosity. In the performance of (innovations on) the masters, doesn't one confirm the successful completion of apprenticeship? And one must wonder if it is false modesty of respectful deference that compels the author to inform us that he has written only 105 essays in his completed collection compared to Montaigne's 107 *Essais*.

Writing less than the admired Renaissance master, in fact, the imitation of a Montaignian gesture that Butor explicitly observed in his *Essais sur les Essais:* Montaigne ceaselessly measured himself against classical standards, often to find himself wanting. In a sense, Butor's adaption of this attitude

---

[1] Michel Butor, «Aux ateliers de la fée Morgane», *Répertoire V* (Paris: les Editions de Minuit, 1982), 315.

situates him in an evolving tradition of consciousness of the inherent limitations of writing and, by extension, of self-consciousness of the limitations of the writer. But there are epistemological complications that become evident in the contemporary writer's work, most particularly, in the «specular moment» of the author seeing himself as an author. As others have queried rhetorically in recent and endless debate: how can language in all its inadequacies be used to describe its own practice? how can knowledge describe itself? In symbolic rather than theoretical fashion, Butor appears to be striking upon this same generic problem — an occupational hazard of writing, so to speak — when he depicts himself as not achieving literary ideals or, more radically, when he does not or cannot depict himself in the act of writing. (He has, of course, regaled us with other «self-portrayals» — student, tourist, observer, bungling vagrant — all of which strategically erode the image of successful writer.) But he categorically refuses us that moment of perfect specularity, of writing about himself as what we empirically know him to be: a writer. Is this a dodge? And does it serve to confirm the existence of this inescapable specular bind? I prefer to interpret Butor's manoeuvering as discovery and acknowledgment of the impasse, which then elicits its own working-through. This «apprenticeship» or, more simply, this learning from one's mistakes accounts for specific developments as well as specific authorial positions in Butor's entire *oeuvre*. Thus I interpret the writer's comparatively early departure from a tradition of self-reflective novels and autobiographical fictions and his subsequent adoption of alternative forms as following a very basic learning pattern of experimenting with failure and then redirecting one's efforts. The odd twist to Butor's apprenticeship is that it progresses from specularity — writing about what one should know best — to a speculativeness — a much more tentative writing activity.

The best-known of Butor's early novels seem to fall into a tradition of first-person, writer's *Bildungsroman* most formidably represented in twentieth century French letters by Marcel Proust. A conventional assesment of *A la recherche* might point to its double narrative deployment of the writer both becoming and being such. The notion of an idealized convergence of apprenticeship and mastery, of the remem-

bered «I» and the remembering «I» within the novel's para-
meters appears to be consonant with the stated Proustian
esthetic: the work of art will create an a-temporal space, give
permanence to otherwise fluctuating subjective states. More
recently, however, critics have focused on the gap between
Proust's «theory» of imaginative synthesis and his actual novelistic practice of discontinuity which results in, as Doubrovsky
represents, a failed quest for identity [2].

Ten years before this critical view came to light, let alone
coming into fashion, Butor was writing the same manner of
self-reflexive novels that consciously set Proustian goals of an
esthetic fusion, consciously adapted a praxis of discontinuity
ostensibly to achieve that fusion, and self-consciously witnessed the failure of both esthetic and subjective goals. (Although
Butor has proven himself to be an excellent reader of Proust [3],
I think it moot to speculate whether the novels are actually
modeled on the *Recherche*.) The question is rather: Are his
novels really failures, or has Butor learned from Proust's mistakes, failing in the same way only better? And might not one
see it as a challenge to the master's faulty theory?

It remains to look at specific novels to assess just how
they fail. The apprentice-writer of *l'Emploi du temps*, for instance, has at his disposal a number of master fictions, most
notably the myth of Theseus and a popular murder mystery
novel. Revel takes these as didactic texts, trying to locate
equivalencies for his own experience. The seductive tale of
Theseus's conquest suggests how Revel might master a language, a culture, a city, and even a woman's love. Here is, indeed,
an ingenuous view of human experience, not to mention writing: perfect iterability is conceivable; students need only
repeat their models. The second text which also rules the
writing of *Emploi*, the detective story, has a particularly desirable feature which is to begin at story's end, filling in the
gaps *chemin faisant*. This helps Revel subscribe to a holistic
view of knowledge and writing; all the elements are there and
discoverable, one need only thoughtfully reconstruct. Revel
thus imagines that the writing process is firmly anchored in a

---

[2] Serge Doubrovsky, *La Place de la Madeleine: Ecriture et fantas-
me chez Proust* (Paris: Mercure de France, 1974).

[3] There are no fewer than four *Répetroire* articles consecrated to
Proust's work.

knowable end. However, the Proustian ideal of a written arte-fact creating the durability and invincibility of a myth or of converting time into an esthetic space accessible at privileged moments is spectacularly disproved: time definitively seals the book off from the literal and figurative space in which Revel could have made discoveries. *Emploi* closes prematurely, that is before the maturation of the writer both in terms of a worka-ble theory of writing and a comprehensive self-knowledge.

Rather than repeat what is similar in the novels, I will merely call attention to the fact that *la Modification* is about an ill-fated attempt at recuperating lost time in very literal ways. More interesting for our purposes are the «modifica-tions» brought to this narrative of apprenticeship. Curiously, despite a relentless thematic of breakdown, gaps, and miscom-munications, the novel sounds a cautious note of optimist. The protagonists' writing of his book will follow upon the expe-rience of failure; it is, thus, the product of experience. By writing, Delmont hopes to pass on what he has discovered in himself, «cette fissure béante en ma personne» [4]. (Even the imaginative terms for specular failure differ between Proust's narrator and Butor's: the former is confronted with multiple subjectivities [5] whereas the latter beholds a split creating an absence.) But Delmont does see a transcendental potential in the reading of his projected book by another character: not to generate a recuperative affective experience, rather to force a realization of what is irrecoverable. Were there better grounds for it, I would accuse Butor of gently satirizing the *Recherche*, shrugging off its euphoric apocalypse with a realist's cynicism.

As though Butor could not escape his modified Proustian model, the last novel, *Degrée*, still experiments with writing against time, to recuperate time ,and to reconstitute self. As before, failing utterly in all this becomes an esthetic and sub-jective crisis, this time in as literal terms as Butor can make them in a fiction (the book becomes an unfinished «ruin» even before the novel ends; and the protagonist internalizes his defeat, yielding himself up to the imminent possibility of total subjective dissolution in the form of death). The struc-tural differences between this novel and its predecessors serve

[4] Michel Butor, *La Modification* (Paris: les Editions de Minuits, 1957), 276.

[5] This is the narrator's admission in the final pages of the *Recherche*.

to underscore certain theoretical advances. First, writing's collapse is located relatively early in the plot. That a different writer continues the book, not to complete it, rather to ensure that it will be read, suggest that writing itself is not a recuperation, but that reading might be. Second, the «writer» experiments with narrational structure, writing from his own point of view, then shifting to the point of view of another character. The «writer's» stated theoretical premises for making this narrational shift are to account more completely i.e., to master better his «subject». But «subject» can also be read as «one subjugated». And indeed, Vernier's relationship to his subject is re-enforced by circumstantial roles of authority: he is uncle and teacher to his subject. The whole practice of writing about and for his pupil-nephew and the role reversals effected narrationally are explicitly intended to liberate his nephew from crushing institutionalism, to teach him not to be its endentured apprentice, to question rote mastery of its values. But this subject-object interchangeability imagined by the writer also recreates a prototype of the specular bind to which I referred earlier. Vernier consciously chooses one level of specularity: his nephew will eventually read about himself. But when Vernier exploits his nephew as informant it creates a second order of specularity in which he can write about and control what is seen and how Vernier himself is seen. (Here lies a latent autobiographical impulse: to be what one writes about.) It is not just romantic tradition or psychological realism or blatant moralizing that compels Butor to dramatize the disastrousness of this writing practice. It is rather emblematic of the failure of theoretical assumption about writing: namely that the reader — at best an accomplice, at worst a stooley — can be manipulated into certain readings and whose collusion, in extreme cases of writerly solipsism, can be dispensed with entirely. Emblematically again, the retrieval (actual by the second reader who writes, hypothetical by the nephew-reader) revises a whole cluster of notions about authority, permanence of experience, and property of experience. And certainly, *Degrés*'s last sentence («Qui parle?») has launched a challenge to authorship and authority that opens the question to real readers.

Of course, precisely at this point in his career, Butor consciously and publicly abandons the relatively sustained narratives of the novel. The non-generic forms that follow quite evidently strive for the decentralization of authority that is theorized about in *Degrée*. Does this suggest some manner of open rebellion against the «masters» of culture and literature? A rhetorical question to be sure. Any reader of Butor has scrambled to understand his knowledgeable and respectful references to culture. For the sake of argument let us take a text that catches the writer in ambivalence towards his cultural masters. *La Description de San Marco* gives tacit nods of acknowledgment in several directions, but no gesture is so odd as the one made towards Proust. He is honored at the book's very limits, on the last cover page:

> Sur cette quatrième page de couverture, dalle du tombeau provisoire que devient le livre au moment où on le referme, comment ne pas commémorer les morts, en particulier le luxueux forçat dans sa fameuse cellule de liège [6].

Only upon closing the book does the reader see that *Description*'s cover serves as «basilica» in the original (medieval) sense of the word: a canopy stretched over a tomb. And in this tomb, to pursue the metaphor, lies buried a literary giant, Marcel Proust. However, I read the tombstone inscription in at least two ways. First, I note that Proust's mortality is commemorated. He is remembered as imprisoned by confining illness in his bedroom-study and as condemned to hard labor by his literary ambitions. And ultimately, he is remembered as dead. It seems that Butor comes to bury Proust, not to praise the immortality of his work. But my alternative reading yields this curious «event»: opening the book lifts away the stone over the tomb, demonstrates the manifest absence of the monument's supposed occupant, as though a reading of this description symbolically resurrected the earlier writer from the dead. In what ways, then, is the master honored, kept alive; in what ways superseded by his disciple?

The mere choice of San Marco is a gesture of tribute to Proust. As Butor has pointed out, Proust liked to think of his

---

[6] Michel Butor, *La Description de San Marco* (Paris: Gallimard, 1963), back cover.

Recherche as an immense cathedral-like structure. For Proust, the cathedral functions as a metaphor subsuming writing. This holistic image, solid and immoveable, sets up a desirable specularity: the cathedral obliquely reflecting the written work with the potential of obliquely reflecting its author. But as noted before, the consolidary force does not extend to the narrator's self-conception. He is not entirely locateable in the monument he has constructed for himself — which is, perhaps, one of Butor's points in situating Proust where he does in the *Description*. There are other signs that *Description* is a revisionary reading of (authors like) Proust. Butor attempts his own conversion of time into a timeless space; as the observer-reader-narrator circulates in the monument, stories and histories appear according to the somewhat arbitrary itinerary of his tour. Instead of writing becoming a monument, the monument becomes readings and, secondarily, writing; it is process rather than product. In a sense this is the execution of a Proustian search to perpetuate something in writing. Take the thumb-nail dramas of desire that Butor stages on this religious site: unfinished, ever-renewable, ever-readable, they are particularly apt in the context of a structure celebrating resurrection, a denial of historical ends and a reassurance of continuity. It could be that this is a revival of Proust's gospel.

On the other hand, Butor certainly cannot be accused of slavish emulation of his model; this despite a meticulous descriptive account that might seem to follow too literally his subject. The resulting description, however, clearly prevents the consolidation of images much less of histories. A single image does not supplant all others; icons are not replaced by icons. Even a floor plan of San Marco cannot remedy the fragmentation of literal and figurative structures. Butor has split apart the image to open the text to further speculation (and this is what is most consistent in all of his texts). Here I wish to proceed carefully. Breaking apart revered images and shattering old myths figures as an iconoclastic gesture. However, concurrent with this act of rebelliousness is Butor's heavy reliance on those same images and texts, as though the most compelling aspect of the warhorses of our culture were that they demand to be re-read and re-construed in a radical way.

It would be false to represent Butor's work since the sixties as not having evolved. But I see his form-shattering technique as something other than an attempt to bedazzle readers with up-to-the-moment avant-gardism. There exists, I contend, a theoretical consistency that also validates the term «apprenticeship» for even his most recent activity. He has deliberately remained a student of texts of various kinds: he writes almost exclusively on, or against, or in concert with, other works and other media. He has consistently maintained a «political» position somewhat counter to that of the institutionalized masters. His projections of himself in writing, even in texts approximating the features of self-portraiture, tend to be playful, fantastic, protean — we are not meant to take their authority too seriously. Butor studiously shuns the pretense of having mastered himself in writing; I suspect the problem with highly specularized writing is that it attempts to reaffirm knowledge that appears to be off limits to the reader. By the same token, Butor refuses in his writing to relinquish the role of reader, of speculator, of undoer of texts. For some, this preference for speculation over specularity, for reading over writing might seem a regression; I think it gives strong evidence of greater mastery and of greater self-knowledge.

Eilene Hoft-March
Lawrence University

ORTEGA Y GASSET: A POETICS FOR THE NOVEL

In Madrid late in July 1914, just days before the storm of war broke out over Europe, young professor of philosophy José Ortega y Gasset published his first volume bearing the title *Meditaciones del Quijote*.

Driven by philosophic, ethnic, political, and aesthetic reflections which added up to the haunting question, «Dios mío, ¿qué es España?» the thirty-one-year-old philosopher undertook a study of *quijotismo* as a means of discovering the national *paideia*. Halfway into his work, however, Ortega concluded his essay, omitting two projected *meditaciones*[1] which seem to have been left unwritten. The essay thus includes only a *Meditación preliminar* and a *Meditación primera*.

In later years the material of the *Meditación preliminar* has been rescued from oblivion by followers of Ortega like Marías and Gaos, who recognized it as the cornerstone of Ortega's later *raciovitalismo*. In this meditation Ortega's famous dictum makes its first appearance: *Yo soy yo y mi circunstancia, y si no la salvo a ella, no me salvo yo.*

The subsequent *Meditación primera*, sub-titled *Breve tratado de la novela*, did not share the same luck, however; for although in its philosophic aspect it was linked to the preliminary meditation, no special literary recognition was bestown upon it except as a somewhat contradictory contribution to Ortega's theory of the novel best summed up in the essay «Ideas sobre la novela», itself a companion piece to the more

---

[1] One of the missing *meditaciones* was to be titled «¿Cómo Miguel de Cervantes solía ver el mundo?» the other, «El alcionismo de Cervantes». See José Ortega y Gasset, *Meditaciones del Quijote, con comentario por Julián Marías*, 2nd. ed. (Madrid: Revista de Occidente, 1966), 183.

famous *Dehumanization of Art*, of 1929, The former was written in answer to a long smoldering controversy over the nature of the novel sustained against Ortega's erstwhile friend and traveling companion Pío Baroja, a major novelist himself and prime Spanish exponent of anything's-a-novel-if-that's-what-you-want-to-call-it school of thought.

Those few who concerned themselves with these things among Spanish literary and art intelligentsia of the Twenties decided to favor Baroja. However much they might admire the young philosopher as a writer and public figure, he was an amateur in questions of practical literary theory and deserved the spanking Baroja had administered in the newspapers [2]. After that, save for a brief article on a novel by Gabriel Miró, Ortega wrote nothing more for years on the novel as an art form. Thus his stock as a critic of the novel sank, and among his writings in that vein which were relegated was his *Breve tratado de la Novela*, inside the *Meditaciones del Quijote*, where, independent of his other writings on the qualities of the novel, he formulated a metaphysics of the novel in its perspective of reality. In Ortega's *tratado*, Cervantes' great work functions as an alternative model from the problem of heroism in real life, as it faces reality, and in the novel, as it faces realism.

In this treatise some of Ortega's statements may seem commonplace to us today, but we must consider the level of academic and literary criticism of the time, 1914, particularly in Spanish letters, which simply was oblivious or ignored the existence of two separate genres for long fictional narratives, romance and novel. In this respect Ortega represented a critical advance, a more European and less narrowly Spanish critical viewpoint [3].

---

[2] See Rodríguez-Luis, «La discusión sobre la novela entre Ortega y Baroja», *La Torre*, 10, núm. 38 (abril-junio, 1962), 85-125. And Carmen Iglesias, «La controversia entre Baroja y Ortega acerca de la novela», *Hispanófila*, núm. 7 (1959), 42-50.

[3] Along with one other important essay written as far back as 1910, Ortega's *Meditaciones* initiates a series of more cosmopolitan considerations on art, literature and aesthetics that will culminate in *La deshumanización del arte*, in 1925. Refer to José Ortega y Gasset, *Obras completas*, III, 5th ed. (Madrid: Revista de Occidente, 1962), 353-420.

For Ortega the critic, epic and novel are opposites. The subjects of the epic lie without communication to the present. They belong to a mythical past that retains an absolute distance from today's realities. The Homeric hexameters, as a case in point, retain an enduring freshness in contrast to our own yesterday and today that soon represent a faded and jaded reality. Our protagonists are not men in the same sense as were Ulysses and Hector, who strove athwart the gods.

So, unlike the novel, whose prime attraction may be its originality, the epic relies on a reworking of the old myths that encompassed the religion, science, and tradition of Homer's day. The story the epic bard had to tell was already known. More than just poetic, his labor was artistic, for his preoccupation lay not so much in plot or character invention but rather in bringing to life and actualizing the known poetic material. His concentration was away from the commonplace reality, not toward it, as is the case with the novelist. From the actual in human existence the epic minstrel grafted into his archaic past only the common terrestial phenomena, like wind and water, beasts and birds. Together they form a common bond with our own cosmos and help actualize distant figures like Achilles and Helen, in themselves unique epic characters. A Madame Bovary, on the other hand, is a novelistic type.

So we see that if the epic represents a virtual past, the novel presents a virtual present. If the epic figures are unique poetic creations, the characters of the novel are typical and extrapoetic. Far from the aesthetic atmosphere of the myth, the latter are taken off the street, from the physical world inhabited by author and reader.

The end of the classic epic period was attended by the separation of science and religion from the myth. In its descent the myth went underground, as it were, to act thereafter as a leavening of fantasy upon history. From the ensuing ferment such figures as Antiochus and Alexander the Great were raised to superheroic dimensions, their fantasized chronicles representing the process of reabsorption of historical fact by the myth, which makes of the former a physical and historical impossibility. Thus the old gods of the myth who hurled their thunderbolts in the epic took up a new address where disorder reigns, the norm is non-existent, and the impossible is possible. For lack of the term *romance* Ortega denotes all literary creation welling up from this spring *la literatura de la imaginación;* and its one article of faith, *Se permite la aventura.*

As a new flowering of this literature from the old epic trunk rode the romance of chivalry straight into the Renaissance. Aside from the brief occasional dialogue in which discreet information is imparted, the poetic instrument of the *romance* or *Libro de caballerías* is the narration, literally the telling of the story. The literature of imagination narrates a past. Its opposite number the novel describes a present.

Already in Cervantes's *Novelas ejemplares* Ortega detected two separate kinds of story. One kind, like *El amante liberal* and *La fuerza de la sangre,* consisted of the aventure tale, replete with amazing exploits and coincidences. This type of story attracts by its fantasy and the heroism of villainy of its characters. In the second kind of tale, on the other hand, as is the case with *Rinconete y Cortadillo* and *El celoso extremeño,* hardly anything exciting happens. As readers we are not compelled so much by their «What happens next?» or by the dynamism of the characters. In fact, we are not so interested in the characters as we are in what they do or what happens to them. Of themselves neither the figures of Sancho Panza or the barber, or the Knight in the Green Cape, or Madame Bovary and her husband, are truly interesting if removed from the context of their stories and presented to us as mere human beings or types. The important point in these characters is the *way* they are presented; herein possibly the foremost underlying distinction that Ortega discerned between novel and romance. Even now, seventy-five years after Ortega's essay, Spanish literary criticism fails by and large to perceive the fundamental difference between two aesthetic intents other than to admit that there are many different kinds of novel, their number and differences being constantly on the increase, as Ortega's literary opponent Baroja proclaimed.

It may be interesting to note, insofar as preference for genre is concerned, that although Cervantes wrote *Don Quijote* as a polemic against the romances of chivalry, nevertheless he did not eschew the role of romancer. Indeed his very last work, the *Persiles* was in that vein. We may therefore conclude in this respect that Cervantes was aware of the fundamental differences in the two genres both in character, already mentioned herein, and in narrative structure. In the latter case romance preserved the epic form of narration in which the more summarily a tale is told and the less is interposed between the event and the audience, the more appealing the story turns out to be. Conversely in the novel the more important structure is not the deed presented directly so much as the scene and the circumstances in which the event is dramatized and the characters represent themselves generally by means of dialogue.

The character of *Don Quijote* himself illustrated the collision of two aesthetic intentions brought into play by Cervantes, one represented by fantasy, the other, by realism. When we follow the adventure tale as it unfolds we experience a growing surge of tension that separates us from reality and bears us with it, like a missile, so that we accept, if but for a moment, the adventure as a reality. Don Quijote represents this type of hallucination in the presence of *Maese* Pedro's puppet show. Streaking along, Don Gaifero's horse gathers into the vortex of its wake the soul of Don Quijote, like a sere leaf. The edge of the stage of *Maese* Pedro's showcase constitutes the border between two spiritual kingdoms. Inside the puppet showcase lies the realm of fantasy wherein the spirit of the myth predominates. Outside, reality reigns supreme. It is here where Don Quijote resides as a borderline character who, although installed in the actual, nonetheless wills to live in the kingdom of fancy. Next to Don Quijote, however, is Sancho, whom Cervantes has posted against all adventure so that the imaginary event, in passing through him, becomes a ridiculous gesture.

For Ortega y Gasset the juxtaposition of these opposing realms produced a third dimension, an advance in which the fantasized poetic plane need no longer abandon the actual in order to exist. Now the imaginary plane becomes secondary and accommodates actual reality, the latter entering the poetic plane so as to elevate the adventure to a higher aesthetic level. And so, even though the realistic novel was born in opposition to romance, still the former bears the essence of adventure within itself. But now the reality of the adventure is reduced, as in *Don Quijote,* to a humor of the mind, indeed, to the psychological. Conceived in irony, the realistic novel neverthe-

101

less requires residually the spirit of adventure that informs romance. The *Quijote,* written as a polemics against the romances of chivalry, sustains within it this opposition. It allows the real and the actual to turn into the substance of poetry, not directly, as in the privilege of the myth, but rather, obliquely as criticism and destruction of the myth. So, in Ortega's own words:

> In this form reality, which is of an inert and insignificant nature, still and mute, acquires movement; it turns itself into an active power of aggression against the crystalline orb of the ideal. The enchantment of the latter having been broken, spent [reality] falls [to earth] as iridescent dust that loses its coloring till it becomes brown soil. In all novels we witness this process so that, speaking rigorously, reality does not become poetic nor does it enter the work of art save only its gesture or movement in which it reabsorbs the ideal [4].

The process, then, is an inversion of romance, with the added difference that the novel describes the process itself, while romance, or the literature of imagination, describes the object produced, the adventure.

As with the windmills that were giants to Don Quijote, we find a duality of interpretation possible to all things. On the one hand those windmills are giants. That is the «idea» or «sense» they impart. Materially, on the other hand, they are windmills. Hence to Ortega the novel encloses a conflict between mind and matter. If the «idea» triumphs and obliterates materiality, we live in a state of hallucination, as did *Don Quijote* at the start of his tilt. But if matter wins and reabsorbs the «idea», we live disenchanted. The latter process represents the victory of realism, which focuses on things in such a way as to underscore their most material aspect. To Ortega the genesis of the modern novel in the *Quijote* is due to the cultural insufficiency that Cervantes the Renaissance man observed about him. All that was noble, idealistic, and poetic in his day was besieged by cruel and brutal reality, just as *Maese*

---

[4] *Meditaciones del Quijote,* op. cit.. 151. Translation ours.

Pedro's puppet show was surrounded by the real world of the inn.

Now where did this brutal realism originate in art? Ortega perceived that it started in imitation, with mime. He who imitates mocks. It was in this spirit that comedy was born. Abandoning the gods and heroes of the myth, Aristophanes took to representing actual people like the ones he bumped into in the market place. Thenceforward the comic intention, taking with it the dialogue as a formal ingredient, evolved till one of its forms ripened into the novel.

Even so, Ortega recognized the tragic side of the novel, having to do with the problem of heroism, straightforward in romance but subdued and dubious in the novel, where it becomes, as in *Don Quijote,* an aspiration in which, though the will to heroism is real, the heroic deed is unreal. Even in our time individuals exist who are resolved not to be content with reality. They aspire to a course of action in life superior to the usual and they refuse to bow to timeworn gestures that habit and biological instinct oblige mass man to make. They are the heroes of our time. And though their intention may lead to tragic conclusions, it is enough to give reality that slight tug sufficient to annihilate all heroism, as we destroy a dream by shaking the dreamer.

The tragic heroism of the novel walks a tightrope. The hero's efforts seem to verge at times on the ridiculous, and the hero is on the borderline of appearing a vulgarly ambitious type. Since the hero's struggle is also a challenge to an entrenched establishment, as it were, the forces of inertia and conservatism react by dispatching realism against him. And he is enveloped in comedy and ridicule. Since heroism is characterized by a will to be, the tragic personage, according to Ortega, has half himself outside reality. It suffices, as noted before, to tug him by the feet all the way to reality for him to become a comic character. In its advance upon the hero, reality reabsorbs the tragic role, making it seem a ridiculous disguise under which mover a commonplace creature. Consequently comedy lives of tragedy as the novel lives of the epic. The distance from the tragic to the comic is the same as from willing to be to believing in being already. Comedy, Ortega reminds us, is the literary genre of conservative parties.

103

Might we say, then, that the book *Don Quijote* was guided by a solely comic intention? Not so, only in its utilization of the poetic significance of the fall of the tragic object, vanquished by reality. The higher line of the novel, for all that, is still tragic. For this reason Ortega considered the novel tragicomedy, a synthetic term that over a century previously Fernando de Rojas had coined for *La Celestina.* In the latter work the gradually evolving genre entered a crisis in its evolution which ripened in *Don Quijote.*

Even though the comic line produces the synthesis of the novel, the tragic line may nevertheless predominate. The species allows for gradations between the two levels. The tragic mode looks straight at the hero. The comic regards him obliquely. The difference, of course, is irony.

Doubtless Ortega recognized that, irony aside, the novel into our day has not stayed fixed as to the proportion of laughter or pain therein contained through changing times. It may have altered its perspective on man and the nature of heroism. But it has not strayed in its essence from the confrontation between idealism and realism. This conflict has remained at the heart of the novel since Cervantes.

Warren Hampton
University of South Florida

RELIGION, ETHNICITY, GENDER: LANGUAGE
MAINTENANCE AMONG MICHIGAN FRANCONIANS

The resurgence of data-based empirical studies in linguistics has led scholars in this country and abroad to focus their attention once again on the few remaining German language islands. In this paper I will trace the role of religion, ethnic pride, and gender as language maintenance factors in one such island — that of the Michigan Franconians — which has never been studied in detail before.

A language island has been defined as a community where at least four fifths of the population are speakers of a minority language which fulfills most communication needs of that community [1]. Generally, such a speech community resides in a geographically delimited territory surrounded by a sea of majority language speakers. Most speech islands which were established in the United States during the 18th or 19th centuries by German immigrant groups shifted to the dominant language during and after World War I, so that those where German is most vital today are associated with sectarian religious groups, such as the Old Order Amish/Old Order Mennonites in Pennsylvania (Pennsylvania Dutch), or the Hutterite Brethren in the Dakotas [2]. To preserve their faith they

[1] Heinz Kloss, «German-American Language Maintenance Efforts», *Language Loyalty in the United States. The Maintenance and Perpetuation of Non-English Mother Tongues by American Ethnic and Religious Groups*. Eds. Joshua Fishman et al. (The Hague: Mouton, 1966), 207.

[2] See for example Marion L. Huffines, «Pennsylvania German: Language Maintenance and Shift», *International Journal of the Sociology of Language*, 25 (1980), 43-58.

Kurt Rein, «Soziokulturelle und sprachliche Wandlungen bei den Hutterern. Beobachtungen anlässlich eines neuerlichen Besuches», *Reli-*

limit contact with the majority culture, and avoid education beyond the 8th grade. Since their language is one of the defining characteristics of their religious and social identity, Standard German is used in the church, while the dialect — either a variety of a single German dialect, or a dialect mixture — is the primary means of communication for all members of the community down to the youngest child. English serves as the link to the outside world. In the case of secular, non-sectarian groups such as the Michigan Franconians, on the other hand, the number of active dialect speakers has declined steadily in the last thirty years or so, and all children are now raised with English as their first language. Therefore, there are no fluent dialect speakers below the age of 40. Concomitantly, the domain of the minority tongue has narrowed considerably, and is now so restricted to the last bastion of dying languages: family, friends and neighbors that it is rarely, if ever, heard in public. Thus, the designation German language island today is applied even to groups where no more than one quarter of the general population are active dialect speakers. The latter tend to be distinguished from those who have shifted to English for all their communication needs by such factors as age, level of education, occupation, degree of ethnic pride, and gender. In order to explain the unusually longer period of language maintenance among the Michigan Franconians in the face of the overwhelming pressure from English their settlement history, of which religion is a vital part, deserves mention here.

The Michigan Franconians inhabit the small township of Frankenmuth — located near Interstate 75 approximately 40 miles north east of Detroit between Saginaw and Flint — and several nearby villages. The communities were established between 1845 and 1853 by orthodox Lutheran immigrants from towns and villages in central Franconia, the area near the city of Nürnberg. Although individual families from other regions in Germany followed during the peak years of German

giöse Minderheiten als Sprachgemeinschaftsmodelle. Deutsche Spra-chinseln täuferischen Ursprungs in den Vereinigten Staaten von Ame-rika. Ed. Kurt Rein. Zeitschrift für Dialektologie und Linguistik. Beiheft Neue Folge Nr. 15 (Wiesbaden: Franz Steiner, 1977), 248-66.

Mark Louden, «Bilingualism and Diglossia. The Case of Pennsylvania German», *Leuvense Bijdragen* 76 (1987), 17-37.

immigration (1860 to 1890) no trace of dialect mixture can be detected as the new arrivals were soon linguistically integrated. Therefore, the Michigan Franconian dialect remains close to the upper east Franconian dialect remains close to the upper east Franconian source dialect in Germany although there is some evidence of morphological simplification, and, naturally, considerable lexical borrowing in the speech of informants. The original purpose for the establishment of Frankenmuth was the conversion of the Chippewa (Ojibwa) Indians, who still inhabited the central part of the state in the mid eighteen hundreds, to the Lutheran faith. Emigration was coordinated by a German Lutheran minister who recruited the potential immigrants, saw to it that they were provided with church funds, and sent them on their way to the Michigan wilderness accompanied by a pastor of his chioce. However, the missions they established soon had to be closed as the Indians migrated further north to escape encroachment by European settlers. Thereafter, the Franconian immigrants devoted themselves to the establishment of a thriving agricultural economy while continuing to adhere to their orthodox Lutheran faith.

The first wave of settlers to Frankenmuth had brought with them a church charter («Gemeindeordnung») which governed all aspects of private and community life, and doubled as the town charter in the new world since the community did not wish to rely on American civil law to resolve disputes of any kind. To provisions were especially instrumental in preserving the ethnic integrity of the community, thus ensuring language maintenance: the first restricted property ownership to Lutherans of good standing in the local congregation, and the second mandated that preaching and teaching would be in German «forever» [3]. Although the charter naturally had no legal force the social climate in this German enclave effectively prevented significant numbers of non-Lutheran English monolinguals from living and working among the Michigan Franconians until the second half of the 20th century.

A few years after their arrival, the Franconian congrega-

---

[3] See «Gemeindeordnung», Archives of the Frankenmuth Historical Association, Frankenmuth, Michigan, I.3.

tions severed all ties with the mother church in Germany after a dispute over doctrinal matters, and joined the German Lutheran Missouri Synod [4], which adhered to the motto that «language saves faith», and required its members to set up a parochial school system. The latter assured language maintenance since it provided bilingual education in Standard German and English. Religious instruction, however, was conducted entirely in German. As a result of rural isolation, the concomitant religious and ethnic homogeneity of the population, and — last but not least — a considerable degree of ethnic pride the traditional trilingualism still maintained by the Amish persisted among the Michigan Franconians much longer than among most other non-sectarian groups. It even survived the propaganda efforts of the 100-percent-American movement which gathered force around the turn of the century, and reached its crescendo during World War I. Until 1940 Standard German was employed in church and school, the dialect in family and community, while English was largely restricted to business relations with members of the majority culture. When the parochial schools ceased providing bilingual education in English and Standard German at the eve of America's entry into World War II English church services began to predominate as younger members, who had become non-literate in their first language, were unable to understand the German sermons. Consequently, in the religious sphere the shift to English, which had been rather gradual up to this point, accelerated. For almost a full century after their emigration from Germany, however, the church was instrumental for language maintenance.

There can be no doubt that the Michigan Franconians perceived themselves as an ethnic group, and were in turn perceived as such by members of the dominant culture. Until the mid-1950's endogamous marriages were still the norm, so that the community had remained largely ethnically homogeneous in the sense that the vast majority of residents were the descendants of 19th century German settlers who shared the same religion and system of values. The virtues of orderliness, cleanliness, hard work, reliability, frugality, honesty,

---

[4] The term German was removed in 1917 in response to the intense anti-German sentiments generated by America's entry into World War I.

self-reliance, and morality were seen as positive characteristics associated particularly with «being German», as opposed to the less exacting standards of the majority culture. Every member of the community, although completely fluent in English, was easily recognized as a Michigan Franconian by his English speaking neighbors since his accent was unmistakably German. Among the youngest group of informants which still practices language maintenance today a positive identification with ethnicity tends to be accompanied by a sense of separateness from the majority culture, a «we» as against «them», which may be expressed during informal sessions with an interviewer.

As late as 1956 the dialect was the first language for many school children [5]. However, as a result of urbanization, a large influx of English speaking residents in the last 30 years, and general socio-economic upward mobility the number of fluent dialect speakers has steadily declined. Currently, the children of active dialect speakers below the age of 50 are bilinguals who are unable or unwilling to produce more than a few stock phrases which they may insert into their English utterances «just for fun». Many parents point out that they deliberately raised their children with English as a second language. The reasons range from having wished to spare the youngsters school entry as German monolinguals to the prevention of the heavily accented English which characterizes the speech of most fluent bilinguals even today. In a number of farm families the children themselves brought about language shift with the parents switching to English in their presence.

All Michigan Franconians over the age of 50 speak and understand the dialect. Fluent dialect speakers between the ages of 40 and 49, however, are generally either farmers of both sexes for whom the minority tongue has remained the dominant medium of communication with friends and family members of their own age and above, or predominantly male non-farmers, often teachers, for whom the dialect constitutes a tie to their community in a fast-changing world. Fluent dialect speakers between the ages of 30 and 39 whose first lan-

---

[5] Donald Beatty, «The Bavarian Dialect in Frankenmuth, Michigan, after a century of American influence», M. A. Thesis, Michigan State University, 1957, 13.

guage was Franconian are few in number. They are almost inevitably male farmers with deep roots in their community for whom dialect use is but one component of their rejection of what they perceive as the negative aspects of modernity. The more strongly a younger male identifies with Michigan Franconian ethnicity the more likely is he to be a fluent speaker of the dialect. Conversely, the more willing he is to leave the community to seek his fortunes elsewhere the greater is the likelihood that he is an English — speaking monolingual with, at best, ap assive knowledge of the dialect. Thus, language maintenance and socio-economic advancement in the dominant culture are non-compatible for younger Michigan Franconians.

Numerous sociolonguistic studies in this country and abroad have demonstrated that women as a group are more sensitive to linguistic norms, and, consequently, tend to shift to the dominant language of language variety sooner than their male age cohorts. Among Michigan Franconians above the age of 50 no gender differences in dialect use can be observed. Between the ages of 40 and 49, however, males clearly predominate numerically among non-farming informants. In spite of diligent search I have, up to now, been unable to discover a single fluent female dialect speaker below the age of 41. This lack of female speakers indicates that the time when dialect use became inappropriate for all but male farm children must have been shortly after 1946 when the Michigan Franconians as a group were becoming less dependent on farming, and the booming postwar industrial economy in nearby cities attracted workers from rural areas. Language shift occurred, then, as a corollary of socio-economic mobility. The small number of women in their thirties who even admit to an interest in the dialect, or who wish they had learned it in childhood often cite the fear of ridicule by fluent dialect speakers, especially males, as one of the deterring factors. In general, however, female informants in that age group who were raised in families where parents and/or brothers are still active dialect speakers evaluate the dialect negahively as a rough and unrefined farmers' language which is, indeed, at times employed in rather earthy contexts. This is not the case for Michigan Franconians of both sexes below the age of thirty for whom the dialect simply no longer has any domain at all. Since it does not concern them personally, dialect use by their elders

110

is not evaluated negatively, but considered to be a quaint remnant of the past.

If religion and ethnicity were the primary factors in language maintenance the gender gap has become the vehicle for language shift since women tend to determine which language is used in the home and with the children. Thus, the last function of the dying Michigan Franconian dialect is as a bonding device for younger males who identify positively with Michigan Franconian ethnicity.

Renate Born
University of Georgia

EÇA DE QUEIROZ AND FLAUBERT

This paper is a deliberate attempt to take Eça de Queiroz out of the context of Portuguese literary history and set him against the backround of the European novel of the late 19th Century. In a sense this is easy to do, because Eça was a diplomat who lived outside Portugal most of his adult life, and as a man of letters he was familiar with the general development of European fiction, especially in English and French. These were the two literatures which had continuous traditions of novel-writing; Eça was well aware of them even before he lived in England and France. During his lifetime the Russian novel, as written by Turgenev, Dostoievsky, and Tolstoi, came into its great prestige, but Eça doesn't seem to have been affected by this momentous development; nor were most of his contemporaries in Western Europe. Nevertheless, as the eminent British critic V. S. Pritchett has remarked, Eça «was responsive to the intellectual forces that were bringing the European novel to the height of its powers» [1]. Pritchett doesn't elaborate this point, but I should like to do so by briefly taking up two of Eça's books.

First, however, I should like to mention the European novelists who provide a kind of setting for this little historical inquiry. Around 1880 —that is the approximate date when Eça's career got underway — there was a rather considerable death toll among these masters. Flaubert and George Eliot died in that year, and they were quickly followed by Dostoievsky, Turgenev, and Trollope. Only Tolstoi among the eminences of this great generation survived, all the way to 1910,

---

[1] V. S. Pritchett, *A Man of Letters: Selected Essays* (New York: Random House, 1985), 253.

but his best novel-writing days were surely over by 1880, and in any case his great fame as a sage had little to do with the fiction of Western Europe. Eça's two most important contemporaries were Emile Zola and Henry James, and it might be interesting to compare these three writers at some length, especially as they were descended from Flaubert. I shall remark here that Henry James, like Eça, had a somewhat ambivalent attitude towards the French realistic novel; in the end both turned away from it. James actually lived in the Paris of Flaubert for a year or so (1875-76), but he rejected this literary milieu for the London of George Eliot and Trollope. Eça was living in England at this same period during the late 1870s, but of course his diplomatic career eventually took him to Paris, which he gradually came to dislike. Both writers, as they grew older, tended to idealize their native countries, Portugal and the United States.

For some of us, in retrospect, the heyday of the European novel was from about 1850 to 1925. This period would include all the writers I have mentioned, plus Thomas Mann and Kafka, Proust and Joyce, a dozen others in several countries. This seventy-five-year stretch of novel-writing could hardly be equalled, not in Europe. The rhythm of creativity has been somewhat slower in the Americas. The United States seemed to come into its full literary powers only during the 1920; and as for Latin America, the last part of the 20th Century is largely theirs. But not everyone would agree with this quick description of literary history. One of the most formidable critics of the last generation was Georg Lukács. In his famous book, *The Historical Novel,* he argues that the strongest period of the novel began at the time of the French Revolution and the Napoleonic Wars, when public events involved the entire European population for the first time and made them aware of the clash of historical forces, of living through certain dates [2]. (I could easily verify this by reference to the English Romantic poets such as Wordsworth.) Sir Walter Scott, hitherto a poet, turned to prose fiction, and his sequence of Waverley novels was a direct response to this shift in sensiblity. As Lukács points out in the first sentence of his book,

[2] Georg Lukács, *The Historical Novel,* trans. Hannah and Stanley Mitchell (London: Merlin Press, 1962).

Waverley appeared in 1814 at almost the moment of Napo-
leon's collapse. From Scott, the key figure in his book, Lukács
moves to Pushkin, to Manzoni, to Fenimore Cooper, to Balzac
and Stendhal. These are some of the great names in the period
of literary history which he celebrates. Then a certain attenua-
tion sets in about 1848, which is of course an important date
in political history for a Marxist. The period that immediately follows is what Lukács calls the «crisis of bourgeois
realism», characterized by a withdrawal of the individual into
private life. Flaubert is the novelist who most brilliantly exem-
plifies this tendency; he is all the more interesting for Lukács
because he wrote a failed historical novel of great artistry,
namely *Salammbô*. Of the writers in Flaubert's generation,
only Tolstoi in *War and Peace* seems to have withstood the
decline in literary power.

The argument here is very impressive in some respects.
Those of us who think of Flaubert as the father of modern
fiction might well consider the ways in which we defend his
literary procedures. I should like to do so by way of Eça de
Queiroz. Eça is the finest of all novelists who immediately
followed Flaubert, and his indebtedness has long been recognized. Alexander Coleman, who has written the major critical
study of Eça in English, has pointed out in some detail the
correspondences between *Madame Bovary* and *O Primo Basílio*. The action of one novel imitates the action of the other
as Eça's heroine Luiza, like Emma Bovary, is punished for her
infidelity. As Professor Coleman remarks, certain episodes in
both novels seem to have been written by the same hand.
Indeed he goes so far as to say that «Luiza's death does not
come with the sense of inevitability and implacability which
accompany the final moments of Madame Bovary... Emma
dies because her world has come apart. Luiza dies only because Emma has died...» [3]. Thus Eça has carried out a formal
literary scheme, probably because he was so impressed by
the original; *O Primo Basílio* is a kind of *hommage* to Flaubert. As Professor Coleman suggests, there is no inner necessity about the action of *O Primo Basílio,* nor is the central
character given the interior life that Emma Bovary has.

---

[3] Alexander Coleman, *Eça de Queirós and European Realism* (New
York: New York University Press, 1980), 119-20.

But *O Primo Basílio* is the early and unrevised work of a writer who would shortly move on to something impressive, namely the third edition of *O Crime do Padre Amaro*, which was throughly revised for its publication in 1880. One might say that this is the year when Eça came into his full strength as a novelist; and one could say the same thing about Henry James, who was just about to publish *The Portrait of a Lady*, his first masterpiece. What a pity that these great contemporaries were unaware of each other's presence, especially when one realizes that Eça was working in England much of the time in England before 1888, when he was appointed consul at Paris. This is the year when he published *Os Maias*, subtitled «Episódios da Vida Romântica».

I am going to suggest that here he follows Flaubert again, but on his own terms. What I have in mind is Flaubert's *L'Education sentimentale* (1869), the first truly modern novel. *Madame Bovary* represents the perfection of a *method* of fiction which so many subsequent writers have acknowledge (most recently Mário Vargas Llosa). *L'Education sentimentale* is an extensión of this method into a much larger scene, the metropolis, Paris, the capital of the 19th Century. As everyone knows, Frédéric Moreau, the central figure, is a sardonius version of Flaubert himself, what Flaubert might have become if he had not acted upon his God-given talent. In writing the novel, Flaubert discovered the modern subject, which might be described as life as a slow and purposeless drift. The action takes us through the Revolution of 1848 and its consequences, but there is nothing decisive about public events, and in the end everyone withdraws into private life. Lukács' general description of the European novel after 1848 is certainly relevant here. It is an epic of a sort, as though much of Balzac's *Comédie humaine* had been condensed into a single narrative, but a narrative composed of fragments or anecdotes.

Os Maias fulfills much the same pattern of narrative. At one time Eça de Queiroz had intended to write a series of twelve novels to be called *Cenas Portuguesas;* this would be his version of Balzac's *Comédie humaine,* with its scenes of provincial and metropolitan life. But this scheme of course never materialized on a large scale; and so he eventually settled for *Os Maias,* surely his masterpiece. It corresponds to Flaubert's *L'Education* in many ways. The central figure,

Carlos Eduardo de Maia, comes from a higher social class than Frédéric Moreau; more is expected of him, especially since his unhappy father killed himself and the ancient line of the Maias seemed to come to an end at that point. His grandfather named him Carlos Eduardo after the last of the Stuart heroes, the claimant to the throne of England, who figures in the Waverley novels of Walter Scott. There is thus a kind of irony about his career from the beginning.

The action of the novel could have been melodramatic, even sensational, because it turns on the theme of incest. Carlos Eduardo's mother ran away from her husband with a lover, accompanied by her infant daughter Maria Eduarda. Many years later Maria Eduarda returns to Lisbon, unaware of her parentage. In the course of the novel her brother meets her and falls in love with her; eventually there is a moment of discovery. But this plot is essentially just the machinery that moves the larger action, because the novel certainly doesn't come to an unhappy end with the discovery of the siblings' relationship. Professor Carol Johnson, in an essay called «Eça de Queiroz: The Arbitrations of Irony», makes the point succinctly: «The tragedy of the book is not the tragedy that readers of *Wuthering Heights* prefer to find. It is a tragedy of dilettantism. Which makes this a very modern book» [4].

Maria Eduarda is inaccesible. She corresponds to Mme. Arnoux in *L'Education sentimentale*, who is inacessible for another reason, namely the fact that she has a husband. In both cases the heroines are presented without the detached critical analysis that is typical of Flaubert and Eça de Queiroz; in a sense their appeal is based on their inaccessibility. Thus unfulfilled passion is part of a sentimental education or a romantic life, to use Eça's subtitle. But the real center of *Os Maias* is Carlos Eduardo's wasted youth, to put it rather bluntly. Talented and rich, he drifts through the society of his time in Portugal without ever finding himself, as we would say nowadays. With a degree in medicine from Coimbra, he expects to do research as well as to go into practice. But nothing ever happens in the beautifully outfitted consulting rooms and laboratory that his grandfather provides for him. He tries the

---

[4] Carol Johnson, *The Disappearance of Literature* (Amsterdam: Editions Rodopi, 1980), 99.

various arts without ever pursuing any one of them with the single-minded ambition that is necessary for success. He has liberal political opinions which, given his social rank and his charming manners, could be the basis for a career in public life. Allowing for different social circumstances, one could describe Frédéric Moreau's life in much the same terms. Carlos Eduardo's friend Ega, who resembles Frédéric's friend Deslauriers in *L'Education*, likewise has grandiloquent literary ideas which provide him with a certain local fame that will never be fulfilled. Even those who are succesful in this bourgeois world — M. Dambreuse the millionaire and his wife in Flaubert's novel, the corresponding figures of Cohen the banker and his wife in Eça's — are scarcely to be envied.

Both novels approach their end in the same way. The famous penultimate chapter of *L'Education* begins:

> He travelled.
> He knew the melancholy of the steamboat; the cold awakening in the tent; the tedium of scenery and ruins; the bitterness of interrupted friendship.
> He came back.
> He went into society. He had other loves still. But the ever-present memory of the first destroyed their savour; and, besides, the violence of desire, the flower of sensation itself, had withered. His intellectual ambitions had also dwindled. Years passed; and he endured the idleness of his mind and the stagnation of his heart [5].

Eça de Queiroz, less sardonic in his presentation, begins *his* last chapter with a newspaper report that Carlos Eduardo, accompanied, by Ega, will begin a long trip around the world in a program very much like Frédéric's. Eventually Carlos Eduardo also comes back and goes into society. He lives for some years in Paris, but in the end he returns to Lisbon. In the last pages of their novels Frédéric and Deslauriers, Carlos Eduardo and Ega, revisit the scenes of their youth; the action simply comes to an end. In *Os Maias* we last see the two friends running along the Aterro at Lisbon, hoping desperately to catch a *bonde* whose red light they have just noticed.

---

[5] Gustave Flaubert, *Sentimental Education*, trans. Anthony Goldsmith (London: Dent, 1941), 389.

Os Maias thus carries out a Flaubertian scheme to a remarkable degree, but it doesn't suffer the comparison at all. For one thing, Eça had seen more of the world than Flaubert; his residence abroad, especially in England, gave him a larger and more genial attitude about human experience. This comes out in his treatment of Carlos Eduardo's grandfather, who has no counterpart anywhere in Flaubert. Then the passage of time is more brilliantly realized in Eça's characters; in this respect he fully anticipates Proust. Eça learned a lot from Flaubert, for instance his use of paragraphing. In Scott and Balzac the paragraphs are great slabs of print, sometimes running to several pages. Flaubert used paragraphs with a new precision; like the details of punctuation, they lead the reader's eye to the continuous shifts in psychological experience. Perhaps this is another way of suggesting that Flaubert introduced a certain intimacy of style, hence perception, into fiction, something that is lacking in Scott and Balzac. Lukács is probably correct in noting the decline in communal experience that seems to occur in the novel after the middle of the 19th Century — «the crisis of bourgeois realism». But the technical gains are considerable, and Eça de Queiroz for one, Proust for another, have an extraordinary power of social analysis, a large vision of experience, that compensates for a lot. I easily join those who consider Eça a European master, and indeed, as I have suggested, during the period 1880 and 1900 only Henry James is in the same category of excellence.

Ashley Brown
University of South Carolina

STRUCTURES MYSTIQUES DE L'IMAGINAIRE
CHEZ FLAUBERT

Bien que l'incroyance de Flaubert en matière de religion soit un fait incontestable, une partie de son oeuvre est clair-semée de grandes images cosmiques ou mystiques. Nous nous sommes proposés d'explorer le dynamisme et la tonalité affective des images contenues dans les *excipit* de la *Tentation de saint Antoine* [1], de la «Légende de saint Julien l'Hospitalier»[2] et d'«Un Coeur simple» [3].

Nous constaterons d'abord que toute vision panthéiste ou mystique, chez Flaubert, a pour origine le besoin de sortir de soi et de s'assimiler continuellement à toutes les formes du non-moi. Cette «viscosité» de l'imaginaire aboutit, sur le plan métaphysique, à la dissolution du moi dans l'univers, et, sur le plan moral, à l'abnégation et à l'amour du prochain. Para-doxalement toutefois, derrière ce détachement du moi, se ca-che, dans le cas d'Antoine, le désir d'une puissance illimitée, et dans le cas de Julien, l'espoir de la reconquête, sur le plan métaphysique, d'une royauté perdue ici-bas. Même dans le cas de Félicité, nous pouvons nous demander si, à l'insu de cette dernière nous n'assistons pas à l'apothéose d'un coueur simple!

C'est dans la *Tentation* que s'exprime le plus directement ce besoin de sortir de soi qui mène à la transcendance. A ses

---

[1] Gustave Flaubert, *La Tentation de Saint Antoine* (Paris: Garnier Flammarion, 1967). Ci-après cité dans le texte de la manière suivan-te: TSA.

[2] Gustave Flaubert, «La Légende de saint Julien l'Hospitalier» in *Trois Contes* (Paris: Garnier Flammarion, 1965). Ci-après cité dans le texte de la manière suivante: LSJ.

[3] Gustave Flaubert, «Un Coeur simple» in *Trois Contes* (Paris: Garnier Flammarion, 1965). Ci-après cité dans le texte de la manière suivante: CS.

débuts, ce mouvement se présente comme une tendance quasi organique, comme Jean-Pierre Richard l'a très bien vu [4]. Cette tendance au glissement vers l'objet, à la fusion avec les êtres finit par se transformer en obsession de la métamorphose. Tous les objets, tous les êtres s'attirent mutuellement et s'assimilent les uns aux autres. Ainsi lisons-nous, juste avant la tirade extatique finale: «Et puis les plantes se confondent avec les pierres (...) Des diamants brillent comme des yeux, des minéraux palpitent» (TSA 251).

Selon Gilbert Durand, qui cite le psychiâtre Minkowski, cette adhésivité de tout sur tout, qu'il apelle parfois «structure gliscomorphe», est caractéristique de l'expression écrite ou pisturale chez les épileptiques [5]. Ceci est d'autant plus intéressant que Flaubert appartient à ce groupe psychologique.

Une autre explication de cette tendance se trouve dans la doctrine du panthéisme, selon laquelle «Il n'y a qu'une seule âme, universellement épandue comme l'eau d'un fleuve divisé en plusieurs bras» (TSA 91). Voilà l'explication métaphisique de cette attirance vers les choses et les êtres! En définitive, le monde est fait d'une seule substance qui change continuellement d'aspect. Le moi et le non-moi ne font qu'un.

Il est intéressant de noter qu'Antoine n'a pas immédiatement saisi la portée de cette définition du panthéisme. Ce n'est qu'à la fin de la *Tentation* qu'il crie son désir de s'assimiler à toute les formes et de circuler à travers toute la création pour en deviner le secret:

> O bonheur! ô bonheur! J'ai vu naître la vie, j'ai vu le mouvement commencer. Le sang de mes veines bat si fort qu'il va les rompre. J'ai envie de voler, de nager, d'aboyer, de beugler, de hurler. Je voudrais avoir des ailes, una carapace, une écorce, souffler de la fumée, porter une trompe, tordre mon corps, me diviser partout, être en tout, m'émaner avec les odeurs, me développer comme les plantes, couler comme l'eau, vibrer comme le son, briller comme la lumière, me blottir sur toutes les

[4] Jean-Pierre Richard, «La Création de la forme chez Flaubert», *Littérature et Sensation* (Paris: Seuil, 1954).
[5] Gilbert Durand, *Les Structures Anthropologiques de l'Imaginaire*, 10.ᵉ ed. (Paris: Bordas, 1984), 311.

formes, pénétrer chaque atôme, descendre jusqu'au fond de la matière, être la matière (TSA 251-252).

Comble de l'insanité? Certes, mais pourquoi ne pas préciser et dire, avec Marthe Robert, que cette phrase extatique reflète surtout le comble de la mégalomanie? [6].

Certains mots-clés, cependant, vers la fin de la tirade, forcent l'attention du lecteur, et demandent à être examinés de plus près: Antoine parle de «*se blottir* sur toute les formes», et émet le voeu de «*descendre* jusqu'au fond de la *matière*» [7]. Cette descente peut être interprétée de diverses façons. D'une part, elle peut signifier la recherche prométhéenne du secret de la création. En ce cas, la *libido sciendi* se confond clairement avec la *libido dominandi*. D'autre part, ce retour *ad originem* trahit peut-être un souhait plus intime. En effet, comme Jung l'afait remarquer, les mots latins *mater* et *materia* ont la même éthymologie (Durand 258). Descendre jusqu'au fond de la matière serait en ce cas une régression sécurisante dans le giron de la *Matière-Mère*, régression que confirme l'image du blotissement foetal. Dans cette optique, la descente exprime le désir d'un retour à létat prénatal et préformel, à «l'en-deça» de l'existence individuelle. Il se pourrait qu'ici les souhaits d'Antoine coïncident avec ceux de Flaubert lui-même. Ce dernier, en effet, avait la procréation en horreur, et a exprimé à plusieurs reprises son regret d'être né et même sa colère de devoir l'existence à l'accouplement fortuit d'un homme et d'une femme. Comment ne pas voir dans cette descente, qui est une remontée dans le temps, le désir d'atteindre le non-temps, afin de se guérir de la souffrance existentielle?

Curieusement, cette longue «hurlade» extatique n'est pas la dernière phrase de la *Tentation*. Flaubert replonge son saint Antoine dans le temps et le ramène à la raison avant de conclure son oeuvre. Les clartés du jour vont ranimer sa foi: il aperçoit la face du Christ dans le disque même du soleil, et se met en prières. Nous assistons ici à un renversement des valeurs: le soleil est sorti victorieux du combat avec la nuit, et la spiritualité l'emporte sur la matière. Le visage du Christ

[6] Marthe Robert, *Roman des origines et origines du roman* (Paris: Grasset, 1972), 333.
[7] C'est moi qui souligne.

auréolé de rayons renforce le symbolisme de la conscience, du «surmoi», déjà présent dans «l'oeil du ciel». Antoine sait qu'il a commis un crime en essayant de retrouver le non-temps au lieu d'accepter l'existence temporelle à laquelle les hommes sont condamnés. Il a, de plus, commis un autre crime, bien plus grave, en tentant de découvrir le secret de la création. Son «surmoi» lui fait des reproches et le rappelle à l'ordre.

Cette soif de puissance, cette *libido dominandi*, nous la retrouvons sous une forme différente chez le saint Julien de la «Légende». Elle s'exprime par le carnage des animaux, et, en particulier, par celui des cerfs, dont les cornes ont toujours symbolisé la puissance virile agressive. Alors qu'il n'est jamais question que d'un unique cerf dans le récits hagiographiques sur saint Julien, Flaubert potentialise à l'infini la puissance que Julien veut faire sienne en multipliant le nombre de cerfs à abattre. Qui peut s'étonner de la prédiction du grand cerf, après un tel massacre? Le carnage des animaux détourne temporairement Julien de son véritable destin; tôt ou tard il l'accomplira.

Nous retrouvons, à la fin du conte, un Julien totalement transformé par la douleur et par une existence dédiée au service d'autrui. Il vit dans une cahute près d'un fleuve aux eaux dangereuses qu'il fait passer aux voyageurs sans demander la moindre rénumération pour ses services. Or, selon Mircea Eliade, la retraite dans une cabane, en pleine forêt, ainsi que l'immersion dans les eaux, symbolisent, dans les rites d'initiation des peuples primitifs, la régression dans le préformel et le retour temporaire à l'indistinct de la préexistence [8]. (Nous avons déjà observé ce retour chez saint Antoine.) L'émersion, par contre, est un symbole de renaissance.

Julien renaît donc à une vie totalement sanctifiée lorsqu'il émerge des eaux avec le lépreux. L'épreuve suprême l'attend dans la cahute, épreuve qui sera immédiatement suivie par l'extase mystique, symbolisée par l'éclatement du toit de la cabane et l'envol dans les airs. Cette double image est une image primordiale dans la pensée religieuse et la philosophie indiennes, que Flaubert connaissait fort bien. La maison qui représente la situation dans le monde, est anéantie. L'image

---

[8] Mircea Eliade, *Mythes, rêves, et mystères* (Paris: Gallimard, 1957), 243.

de l'éclatement du toit signifie qu'on a choisi la liberté absolue, et ce choix implique le reconcement à tout le monde conditionné [9].

En acceptant par charité de réchauffer la chair pourrie du lépreux, Julien retrouve honneur et gloire sur le plan métaphysique. La métamorphose du lépreux en Christ gigantesque, la transformation de ses cheveux en rayons lumineux, l'envol de Julien dans ses bras vers la pureté des espaces bleus, tout proclame la victoire de l'esprit sur la chair et la participation du réprouvé à la puissance du Très-Haut. Alors que cette souveraineté était prise d'assaut par Antoine, elle est accordée à Julien en tant que récompense pour avoir su reconnaître et assumer, dans la misère particulière du lépreux, la misère de la condition humaine.

Nous retrouvons la structure de l'inversion des valeurs dans l'excipit d'«Un Coeur simple». C'est l'imagination de Félicité qui transfigure ses derniers moments, comme elle a toujours transfiguré la réalité de sa vie. Après s'être dépossédée du perroquet empaillé pour en orner le reposoir, elle attend l'arrivée de la procession sous ses fenêtres. Devenue aveugle, elle n'est pas consciente de la déchéance du perroquet, dont Flaubert nous a fait la description: «Bien qu'il ne fût pas un cadavre, les vers le dévoraient; une de ses ailes était cassée, l'étoupe lui sortait du ventre» (CS 80). Lorsque la procession arrive, Félicité entre en extase; le piètre objet de son amour est transformé en un perroquet gigantesque, «planant audessus de sa tête». La gigantisation et l'élévation de l'oiseau à un niveau très supérieur à celui du reposoir où on l'a «caché sous des roses» font de lui un être désanimalisé et tout-puissant aux yeux de Félicité que la cécité a rendue visionnaire.

Si nous continuous à comparer la fin de ce conte à celles de la Tentation et de la «Légende», nous sommes bientôt frappés par l'absence du personnage principal dans le ciel où plane le perroquet. Alors qu'Antoine, en adhérant à tout, emplit le cosmos de sa présence et que Julien (plus modeste) participe à la gloire du Créateur, Félicité reste bien à plat sur non5 lit. L'effacement du moi est-il si complet chez Félicité qu'elle ne peut concevoir l'idée de partager la gloire

---

[9] Mircea Eliade, *Le Sacré et le profane* (Paris: Gallimard, 1965), 150.

du perroquet divinisé?» [9]. Elle possède pourtant à un très haut degré cette fameuse «faculté panthéiste» que Flaubert appelle aussi «illusion» ou «imagination» dans sa *Correspondance*. Cette imagination lui a même procuré, comme à Flaubert, plus de joie que la réalité. La communion de Virginie l'ébranle bien autrement que la sienne!

Si Félicité devient Virginie au moment de la communion de cette dernière, sans doute devient-elle Loulou lorsqu'il subit sa glorieuse transformation. Loulou n'est-il pas devenu pour elle «un fils, un amoreux», avec lequel elle échange des «mots sans plus de suite» qui n'ont de sens qu'au niveau affectif? Comme Debray-Genette l'a indiqué, Flaubert établit tout un réseau de rapports métonymico-métaphoriques entre Félicité et le perroquet [10]. Ainsi, lorsque celui-ci se cramponne à son fichu et qu'elle branle la tête, «les grandes ailes du bonnet et les ailes de l'oiseau [frémissent] ensemble» (CS 70). Dans une des versions qui ont précédé la version finale de l'*excipit*, Flaubert va jusqu'à écrire: «La couleur de sa peau grise [était] semblable à la couleur des pattes du perroquet» (Debray-Genette 110). Bien que cette phrase ait été omise de la version définitive, elle mérite d'être citée à titre d'exemple frappant de la viscosité de l'imaginaire flaubertien: la couleur des pattes de Loulou *déteint* sur la peau de Félicité.

C'est cette même structure gliscomorphe qui est à l'origine de la confusion, dans l'esprit de Félicité, entre perroquet et Saint-Esprit. Trouvant une ressemblance entre Loulou et l'oiseau représentant le Saint-Esprit sur une image d'Epinal, Félicité contracte l'habitude idolâtre de dire ses oraisons agenouillée devant le perroquet. Le Saint-Esprit et le perroquet ne font qu'un. Or, nous venons de voir que Félicité, à l'heure de sa morte, est parvenue à faire entrer son âme dans la Grand Ame de l'univers.

Naïve ou complexe selon le personnage, la vision cosmique contenue dans chacun des trois *excipit* que nous venons d'étudier est l'aboutissement naturel de cette structure gliscomorphe qui unit, relie, et rattache tout à tout. Ajoutons que, pour qu'il y ait spiritualisation de l'être, il faut qu'il y ait non seulement détachement du moi mais aussi renoncement au monde condi-

[10] Raymonde Debray-Genette, «"Un Coeur simple": Ou comment faire une fin» in *Gustave Flaubert I* (Paris: Lettres Modernes, 1984), 110.

tionné. Or, comme nous l'avons vu, l'inversion des valeurs et des situations fait suite instantanément aux actes de renoncement et de charité; le corps de Loulou mangé par les vers ainsi que le corps du lépreux se transforment en corps célestes et glorieux. Nous retrouvons également cette structure de l'inversion dans l'*excipit* de la *Tentation,* sous une forme plus complexe. C'est à un véritable changement de *régime* que nous assistons. En effet, nous voyons tout d'abord Antoine descendre jusque dans la matière. Cette descente, qui n'est pas une chute mais un retour nostalgique à un état préformel et atemporel, est caractéristique du *régime nocturne* de l'imaginaire, selon Durand. La nuit et les quiétudes de l'intimité y sont valorisées. Par contre, lorsque l'invincible Christ solaire surgit à l'horizon, les valeurs du *régime diurne* detrônent celle du *régime nocturne.* Le surmoi résiste à la montée des instincts, et dicte son devoir à Antoine.

En conclusion, il semble bien qu'en montrant l'envers et l'endroit des êtres et des situations, Flaubert ait trouvé ce fameux point de l'esprit dont parle André Breton: «... d'où la vie et la mort, le réel et l'imaginaire, le passé et le futur, le communicable et l'incommunicable, le haut et le bas, cessent d'être perçus contradictoirement...» [11].

Helene Cassou-Yager
Georgetown University

[11] André Breton, *Second Manifeste du Surréalisme* (Paris: Edition du Sagittaire, 1947), 11.

FOLIE, VIOLENCE ET LANGAGE DANS
LE PROCES-VERBAL DE J. M. G. LE CLEZIO

Le procès-verbal, le premier roman de J. M. G. Le Clézio paru en 1963, raconte comment Adam Pollo tente plusieurs expériences dangereuses qui le conduiront aux portes de la folie. C'est à travers le récit des tribulations métaphysiques de ce jeune homme audacieux que l'auteur explore les possibilités du langage humain. Il place son héroes à la croisée de deux chemins représentant les deux langages dont l'homme pourrait se servir: le premier, le langage conceptuel, celui des clichés et des lieux communs, entrave l'homme et l'empêche de saisir la réalité et d'en exprimer la totalité et le second, le langage adamique ou substantiel qui lui permettrait, sinon d'aprivoiser la réalité du moins d'en dévoiler la multiplicité.

La première partie de mon exposé montrera que Le Clézio dénonce l'inefficacité du langage conceptuel dès le début du roman et que le jeune Adam en constitue l'incarnation mythique. La deuxième partie décrira comment Adam tente de se libérer des contraintes du langage conceptuel qui le force à accepter une vision préconçue du monde et à exprimer en clichés. La troisième partie analysera les conséquences que l'audacieuse entreprise métaphysique du jeune Adam a entraînées et en étudiera la signification symbolique. Enfin la conclusion soulignera que Le Clézio a contribué de façon très originale à la brûlante question du langage, et que, s'il n'a pu y répondre de manière définitive, il a du moins cherché à la poser à nouveau avec plus de force et d'insistance que jamais.

1. INEFFICACITE DU LANGAGE
   CONCEPTUEL

Le Clézio intitule son roman «procès-verbal» et attire ainsi l'attention de son lecteur sur le propos de ce roman: le «procès-verbal» désigne le fait de parler, de «verbaliser». L'auteur cite d'ailleurs *Robinson Crusoé* au début de son récit et réaffirme ainsi que le problème du langage joue un rôle essentiel dans son roman:

> Mon perroquet, comme s'il eût été mon favori, avait seul la permission de parler (7).

Seul, le perroquet a le droit à la parole... Celui qui parle comme un perroquet souffre de psittacisme, c'est-à-dire qu'il «raisonne sans avoir les objets mêmes de l'esprit... [qu'il] récite sur la foi d'autrui» (Cuvillier 150). En évoquant le perroquet, une image également chère à l'auteur du *Dictionnaire des idées recues*, Le Clézio dénonce l'aspect mécanique du langage conceptuel fait de lieux communs qui ont perdu leur signification essentielle. Cette image du perroquet, Le Clézio la reprend dans son roman et l'associe à Adam, le personnage du *Procès-verbal*:

> Adam regardait leurs lunettes noires et il imaginait qu'au lieu d'aller vivre tout seul dans son coin, il aurait pu faire quelque chose d'autre: par exemple, *acheter un perroquet* qu'il aurait porté tout le temps sur son épaule, en marchant; de sorte que si on l'avait arrêté, *il aurait pu laisser le perroquet dire pour lui:*
>
> «Bonjour comment ça va?»
> «Bonjour comment ça va?»
>
> et les gens auraient compris qu'il n'avait rien à leur dire (109).

Adam, le héros du *Procès-verbal,* refuse d'utiliser le langage conceptuel, une institution sociale dont se servent les hommes pour communiquer entre eux. Adam ne veut plus le parler parce que la vie précède l'acte de verbalisation. Dans un long monologue, il explique à son alter ego Michèle qu'il a l'impression de falsifier la vie, de la figer, quand il se sert de ce langage:

«Quelle heure est-il?... Est? L'existence; encore un mot, un anthropomorphisme par rapport à l'abstrait, dans la mesure où l'existence est la somme des sensations synesthésiques de l'homme... Si tu savais comme elle me torture cette petite phrase! Ou plutôt non. C'est moi qui en souffre. Je suis écrasé sous le poids de ma conscience. J'en meurs... (69-70).

Dans ce passage, Le Clézio met en question toute la pensée occidentale qui prétend qu'«au commencement était le Verbe» et que le langage est la réalité. Adam refuse catégoriquement d'observer le monde à la manière du cartésien et préfère le contempler à la façon de son homologue du paradis terrestre: ce personnage, passionné d'absolu, désire entreprendre une double recherche métaphysique: il vise à une connaissance intuitive du monde et il cherche à l'évoquer de façon intelligible.

Le langage conceptuel prétend pouvoir expliquer la réalité alors qu'en fait il l'annihile totalement. Adam conçoit l'existence d'un autre langage dit substantiel qui exprimerait la vie sans la restreindre. Les hommes utilisent le langage conceptuel parce qu'ils vivent en société et qu'ils doivent pouvoir communiquer entre eux. Adam comprend encore parfois ce langage codé, il l'utilise quand il descend en ville pour acheter des provisions ou quand il parle avec son amie Michèle. Pourtant ce langage est aliénant parce qu'il est vide et mécanique comme celui du perroquet. Adam en perd lentement l'usage parce qu'il ne s'en sert plus que très rarement: il s'en détache d'autant plus rapidement qu'il s'infiltre de plus en plus dans la sensibilité d'autres êtres afin de saisir la réalité dans toute sa multiplicité.

2. LES TRIBULATIONS METAPHYSIQUES D'ADAM POLLO

Adam se transforme mentalement en plusieurs animaux au cours du roman, en chien, lion, rat ou ver de terre. Dans son roman, Le Clézio décrit, à plusieurs reprises et de façon très détaillée, la lente période d'initiation qu'Adam doit subir avant d'atteindre l'inconscience. Il en trace l'évolution, au chapître «F» du roman, dans l'épisode du zoo, où Adam passe tout un après-midi devant la cage aux lions. C'est d'ailleurs dans cet épisode que se dégagent le plus clairement les trois phases que le jeune homme parcourt lors de son évolution mentale. La première se situe an niveau sensoriel où domine l'odorat: Adam commence par renifler»... les odeurs multiples qui se dégageaient du fumier et des fauves» (82). Cette première phase lui procure une certaine volupté qui le prépare à l'étape suivante, celle de la sensualité. Les sens éveillés, le jeune homme fait appel à son imagination et s'invente toute une série d'images érotiques: «il pensa que la lionne aurait pu être une femme» (82). La concentration intense des deux premières phrases plonge le jeune Adam dans une sorte de passivité langoureuse, caractéristique de la troisième et dernière phase: «il se laissa envahir par une torpeur où dominait le désir de toucher la fourrure [de la lionne]...» (83). Ainsi Adam atteint-il le niveau de l'inconscience où domine l'instinct pur: c'est à ce moment-là que la sensibilité d'Adam vibre des expériences de la réalité authentique qui lui procurent un «plaisir délicieux» (85).

Après avoir fait l'expérience de cette contemplation «inhumaine» de la réalité, Adam tente de la communiquer aux autres. Il tient un discours incohérent dans un jardin public et se fait arrêter puis interner à l'hôpital psychiâtrique pour «exhibitions qualifiables d'attentat à la pudeur (255). Le Clézio se contente de mentionner les incidents qui mènent à l'arrestation de son protagoniste dans une coupure de journal reproduite telle quelle dans le texte du roman. Il ne fournit guère non plus d'explication à propos de l'attentat à la pudeur qu'Adam aurait commis, il y fait simplement allusion et nous pouvons spéculer qu'Adam s'est probablement dévêtu en public. Cet acte déraisonnable a une portée symbolique: il révèle qu'Adam ne comprend plus les conventions d'une société que la nudité embarrasse parce qu'elle se fonde précisément sur l'affirmation que les hommes sont des êtres raisonnables et non des animaux.

3. FOLIE ET VIOLENCE D'ADAM POLLO

Adam s'isole lentement de ses contemporains parce qu'il se laisse envahir, de plus souvent, par une fascination grandissante pour le monde biologique. Il perd ainsi toute perspective humaine et sociale, tout sens du langage conceptuel:

> A force de voir le monde, le monde lui [Adam] était complètement sorti des yeux... il était devenu mémoire... C'était l'endroit, voisin de la vision totale, où il arrive qu'on ne puisse plus vivre, plus jamais vivre (89).

Les hommes ont oublié le langage substantiel en se civilisant et en s'organisant en société mais Adam s'y débat substantiel parce qu'il veut pouvoir exprimer la réalité de façon intelligible. Il n'y parvient malheureusement pas. Quand il écrit dans ce langage, nous ne pouvons le comprendre. Le Clézio nous le montre très clairement quand il cite des extraits du journal intime d'Adam. Ces extraits sont incohérents, dépourvus de sens, pleins de blancs, chargés de ratures, de mots illisibles ou de phrases inachevées. Quand il parle ce langage, les gens ne le comprennent pas et le traitent de fou.

Le langage substantiel est mystérieux et terrifiant: celui qui veut le maîtriser court le risque de s'aliéner de la société, de devenir muet, de débiter des incohérences ou d'exhiber un comportement déraisonnable, asocial. C'est précisément ce qui arrive au jeune Adam: il erre sans but dans la ville, suit un chien pendant des heures, prétend acheter des disques qui n'existent pas, se dispute avec des étrangers dans un café, prononce des discours insensés et viole son amie Michèle. Il perd aussi l'usage du langage conventionnel et la faculté de raisonner, agit par pur instinct et succombe à la violence.

Adam commet deux actes extrêmement violents dans le roman: il tue sauvagement un rat et viole brutalement son amie Michèle. Dans son récit du premier acte violent d'Adam, Le Clézio détaille soigneusement la métamorphose intérieure du jeune homme et décrit minutieusement les différentes étapes de cette transformation. Le jeune homme réussit tellement bien dans son désir de ressentir le monde biologique qu'il s'identifie littéralement au rat qu'il voit devant lui: il parvient à s'élever au niveau de l'inconscience, se laisse dominer par ses instincts et finit par tuer le rat dans un accès irrationnel de rage folle:

> Arcbouté sur ses quatre pattes. Adam avançait en criant, en grognant, en marmonnant des injures: les mots n'existaient plus... Adam était perdu en plein abstrait; il vivait, ni plus ni moins: il lui arriva même de couiner (122-23).

La violence d'Adam est totale dans cette scène. Le jeune homme est littéralement hors de lui, il se trouve à la limite de l'expérience humaine et ressent le monde biologiquement («il vivait, ni plus ni moins»): il reste rat, il ne parle plus, il couine. Le Clézio insiste d'ailleurs sur la déshumanisation qu'Adam subit lors de l'exécution du rat en opposant, aux «mots» du rat supplicié, les cris inhumains du tortionnaire (122): c'est en perdant la faculté de se servir du langage conceptuel qu'Adam perd son humanité.

La deuxième scène, celle du viol de Michèle est intéressante parce que c'est Adam lui-même qui la raconte et qu'il cherche à déterminer le mobile de son acte:

> Je crois que je faisais tout sans savoir, n'importe comment... Et en principe je t'ai violée comme ça, facilement, tu vois, trempée de pluie comme dans une baignoire... Mais, après tout, ce n'est peut-être pas tellement important pour moi. Du moment que j'avais réussi à te mettre toute nue (139-40).

Le jeune homme n'arrive pas à justifier cet acte et reconnaît qu'il a agi purement instinctivement. Il insiste sur la gratuité de l'acte qu'il a commis: la morale de la société et les implications sociales de cet acte ne l'affectent guère parce qu'elles font partie de la réalité sociale que le langage conceptuel crée et que le jeune homme rejette dans son désir d'absolu. C'est pourquoi il est furieux quand Michèle lui dit qu'elle avait pensé déposer plainte contre lui. Cet acte de violence fait partie de la mission qu'Adam a décidé de remplir et ne relève donc pas de la morale de la société qui entrave sa liberté d'homme à la recherche de l'impossible.

Adam se rend parfaitement compte qu'il est capable de se livrer à la violence, à la brutalité et parfois même à la cruauté. Pourtant il ne cherche pas à y remédier: la fascination qu'il éprouve, quand il ressent les vibrations du monde biologique, le remplit d'un singulier vertige qui l'empêche de se maîtriser. Le jeune homme est également conscient du fait que sa recherche métaphysique pourrait devenir dangereuse. Il accepte cependant d'en subir les conséquences, fût-ce au péril de sa santé mentale: ainsi écrit-il «Adam Pollo, martyr» sur la couverture de son journal intime, le fameux cahier jaune dans lequel il ne cesse de relater ses expériences métaphysiques (226). Sans doute le jeune homme pressent-il également qu'il ne peut éviter ni la violence ni la folie dans sa recherche de l'absolu.

La violence constitue par conséquent la ligne de démarcation entre le monde humain et inhumain: elle prive Adam de son humanité, de son sens social. C'est pourquoi ce jeune homme considère la société comme hostile, programmée, mécanique, semblable au monde des fourmis. Adam a entrevu un monde radicalement inhumain dont l'homme est absent, il est parvenu à transgresser les limites de la raison et s'est laissé envahir par la vision d'un monde apocalyptique qui s'achemine fatalement vers le néant. Adam a goûté au fruit défendu, celui de la connaissance intuitive de son homologue du paradis terrestre, et s'est ainsi banni du jardin de la Raison... La violence est le prix que l'homme paie pour avoir osé franchir le seuil de son entendement. L'autre prix à payer, c'est la folie ou la dé-raison telle que la société la conçoit... un prix qu'Adam paie aussi chèrement puisqu'il est envoyé à l'asile psychiâtrique où il «n'attend plus rien ...Il vit énormément... Il va dormir vaguement dans le monde qu'on lui donne... Il est dans l'huître, et l'huître au fond de la mer» (314).

CONCLUSION

Dans son roman *Le procès-verbal*, J. M. G. Le Clézio est parvenu à recréer le mythe légendaire du langage substantiel qui exprime la réalité dans toute sa totalité. Il invente Adam Pollo, «le premier et le dernier homme», qui apprend à écouter le monde, à en entendre les vibrations secrètes, et qui finit par succomber à la puissance de son expérience métaphysique. L'auteur évoque ainsi, de façon poignante, la recherche que certains poètes du passé ont entreprise au péril de leur vie et de leur art poétique. C'est ainsi qu'il réussit la gageure d'écrire une oeuvre lumineuse où se pointe tout à coup la possibilité d'effleurer l'absolu à la surface des mots.

OEUVRES CITÉES

Cuvillier, Armand: *Nouveau vocabulaire philosophique*, Paris: Armand Collin, 1969.
Le Clézio, J. M. G.: *Le procès-verbal*, Paris: Gallimard, 1971.

Rose-Marie Kuhn-Zinda
California State University, Fresno

SIGHT AND INSIGHT: A LOOK AT VISION
IN PASCAL

Blaise Pascal means more things to more readers than most authors in the canon. Here he is a fundamentalist retrograde, there a bold and daring modern; here a brilliant stylist, there a predictable ideologue; a fanatic; a saint. Over the modest course of this study, Pascal will show another face, that of a visionary — not the one to envisage the *machine d'arithmétique,* the *carrosses à cinq sous,* the treatise on the *roulettes* or a solution to the *carrés magiques* — but, rather, someone whose writings are laced with expressions of vision. Indeed, it could well be argued that across the body of his work Pascal's deepest design is to persuade an often adversarial or resistant reader to abandon a complacent blindness and to look intently upon the evidence of truth [1].

In Pascal's work on the void, to take an especially pertinent series of examples, the place of evidence, of that which presents itself directly to the eyes (evidence, from *videre* = to see), will, logically, be of basic import. On this question of the void, the most pressing task facing Pascal is, in a very real sense, more rhetorical than scientific. He must effect the conversion of a generally hostile readership nourished — one could say malnourished — on the Aristotelian assertion that nature, in its abhorance of the void, would implode were a a void to occur. He needs, then, to prove the existence of something that had been invested with the status of counter-

---

[1] «Les chiffres confirment combien il est essentiel pour Pascal de voir et de faire voir. C'est par là qu'il fait passer toute connaissance. Aucune abstraction ne peut pénétrer dans son esprit sans transposition visuelle». Michel Le Guern: *L'image dans l'oeuvre de Pascal* (Paris: Klincksieck, 1983), p. 158.

matter [2]. To do this, he will have to render visible that which is invisible; or, more precisely, he will have to render visibly invisible that which has been explained (away) as invisibly visible. Confronted with the evidence of an apparent void at the top of a tube filled with mercury inverted into a tub containing mercury and water, the opponents of the possibility of the void maintain that the empty spaces is in fact occupied by «des esprits de mercure; d'un grain d'air imperceptible raréfié»; by what Pascal's judges to be «une matière qui ne subsistait que dans leur imagination» [3].

Now, while these positions may vary as to the degree of rarefication attributed to what is *not* seen at the top of the tube, the proponents of the impossibility of the void all maintain that something material *clearly* inhabits the empty space. There would be no empty spaces, no holes in their argument. Moreover, the plenitude (of the space and of the argument) would be guaranteed by what Pascal refers to as the mental power of the subtle: «[...] et tous, conspirant à bannir le vide, exercèrent à l'envi cette puissance d'esprit, qu'on nomme Subtilité dans les écoles, et qui pour solution des difficultés véritables, ne donne que des vaines paroles sans fondement») [4]. Pascal's term not only invokes in an ironic way the *matière subtile* subscribed to by Descartes and others, it serves also to invite the attentive reader to consider the thin weave, the tenuous textuality of argument opting for blindness over insight, of authority over reason. The term *subtile* derives from *sub* and *texere,* the second component being linked etymologically to the notion of *technique*. The subtle technique would be a cloudy technique pronouncing itself clear and evident. However, the words put forth to express that technique are without bottom of foundation. One cannot get to the bottom of the issue precisely because an obstructive screen of subtle matter is made to occupy the *vide en apparence*. Correlatively, the words Pascal's adversaries use to define their position will

---

[2] Pascal's own conception of the *vide,* as he explains it in his «Lettre à M. Le Pailleur au sujet de Père Noël, Jésuite», is that it occupies the middle ground between «la matière» and «le néant».

[3] Blaise Pascal: «Expériences nouvelles touchant le vide» in *Oeuvres complètes,* ed. Jacques Chevalier (Paris: Pléiade, 1954), p. 363. With the exception of the *Pensées,* all references to Pascal's works will be to this edition.

[4] Pascal, p. 363.

often tend to advertise their own circumlocutional heaviness and lack of clarity. Their effort to fill the void would, in Pascal's eyes, be as much an effort to fill the void of faulty thinking.

Pascal's most basic plea, then, is that his rivals accept the reality of that which appears directly to the mind's eye, to the eye whose function is to follow and accede to the enlightenment afforced by proper scientific methodology [5]. Pascal is persuaded that his methodology has in fact shown, has presented clearly to the intellectual eye the reality of the *vide:* «[...] j'ai montré que le vide en apparence, qui a paru dans les expériences, est vide en effet de toutes les matières qui tombent sous les sens, et qui sont connues dans la nature» [6]. What comes into appearance consequent to orderly methodology is nothing other than fact. It is what Pascal calls «le solide»; that is, what impinges itself on the understanding by offering the kind of resistance by which sight and insight can focus and orient themselves. Pascal's *solide* can, therefore, be put in functional juxtaposition with the solidity of materiality his adversaries would purport to «see» in the so-called void. Pascal's *solide* is clear and transparent precisely because it comes of a clear and orderly scientific approach.

What comes of disorderly methodology is perhaps best expressed in the Jesuit Noel's blinding definition of light: «La lumière est un mouvement luminaire de rayons composés de corps lucides, c'est-à-dire lumineux» [7]. The lack of lucidity characterizing the definition is fully analogous to the lack of lucidity on the experimental level. Pascal's objection to this sort of obfuscation is that the terms being used to generate a definition are themselves in need of defining. Any derived

---

[5] In his probing and provocative study, *L'Horreur du vide* (Paris: Editions du C.N.R.S., 1978), Jean-Pierre Fanton d'Andon argues that Pascal's much touted experimental approach to the *vide* was anything but scientific. For the purposes of this study we will nonetheless posit the concept of proper methodology as an ideal to which Pascal aspires at least in principle. By the same token, we will discuss his approach to and preconceptions about Catholicism as ideals, not truths, informing Pascal's modes of thinking.

[6] Pascal, p. 364.

[7] «Lettre de Blaise Pascal au très bon Révérend Père Noël», in Pascal: *Oeuvres complètes,* p. 377.

definition can only be as clear as the terms that would articulate that definition [8].

For Pascal, the essential is to look and to look for; its is to train the intellectual eye in a non-prejudiced way on the possibility of something that may have once seemed beyond the compass of vision. In this regard, the argument tendered by Pascal in his *Préface pour le traité du vide,* is particularly appropriate. As part of his argument in favor of an *enlighte*-ned approach to those areas of intellectual pursuit governed by reason and research, Pascal insists that nature's secrets are merely hidden; and that it is a matter of discovery, of uncovering, contemplating and assimilating that which will inevitably show itself to the unprejudiced (re)searcher. What is more, research and discovery would be ongoing activities-activities that he characterizes aptly in terms of vision. If the knowledge of the ancients can be considered qualitatively as sound as ours, the extent of their knowledge was meaningfully limited by a less developed sense of vision: «*Notre vue a plus d'etendue,* et, «quoiqu'ils [the ancients] connussent aussi bien que nous tout ce qu'ils pouvaient remarquer de la nature, ils n'en connaisaient pas tant néanmoins, et *nous voyons plus qu'eux*».

Pascal will corroborate this claim of the extended power of sight enjoyed by the moderns by turning to the most appropriate example of the telescope. The ancients could not be held accountable for their short-sightedness regarding the Milky Way. To their eyes, the Milky Way had necessarily to appear solid. On the other hand, it would be inexcusable for the moderns to maintain the same view when with the aid of the *lunette d'approche,* the true character of what had seemed solid can be brought into clearer focus. The local application of this point, of course, is that the solidity of the material

---

[8] «Cette véritable méthode, qui formerait les démonstrations dans la plus haute excellence, s'il était possible d'y arriver, consisterait en deux choses principales: l'une, de n'employer aucun terme dont on n'eût auparavant expliqué nettement le sens; l'autre, de n'avancer jamais aucune proposition qu'on ne démontrât par des vérites déjà connues; c'est-à-dire, en un mot, à définir tous les termes et à prouver toutes les propositions». Pascal: *De l'Esprit géométrique* in *Oeuvres complètes,* p. 577. For an important discussion of this work, see Hugh Davidson, *Audience, Words and Art* (Columbus: Ohio University Press, 1965).

supposedly contained in the tube above the mercury is not at all what the proponents of the ancient view had proposed to «see».

The lessons of looking, so integral to Pascal's physics, will apply also and in a statistically meaningful way to his apologetic writing. Indeed, in one of the most celebrated fragments of the *Pensées*, Pascal will bid his reader to gaze not at the Milky Way, but at the sun. «Que l'homme contemple donc la nature entière dans sa haute et pleine majesté, qu'il éloigne sa vue des objets bas qui l'environnent. Qu'il regarde cette éclatante lumière [...]» [9]. The visual and visionary voyage that Pascal urges his reader to take is designed specifically to make that reader face the evidence not just of his disproportion but also of his inability to see: «*incapable de voir* le néant d'où il est tiré et l'infini ou il est englouti».

The fragment immediately preceding the one on the disproportion of man is shot through with references to sight:

> En *voyant l'aveuglement* et la misère de l'homme, en *regardant* tout l'univers muet [...], j'entre en effroi [...] *Je vois* d'autres personnes [...] Je leur demande s'ils sont mieux instruits que moi. Ils me disent que non et sur cela ces misérables égarés, *ayant regardé* autour d'eux et *ayant vu* quelques objets plaisants s'y sont donnés et s'y sont attachés. Pour moi je n'ai pu y prendre d'attache et considérant combien il y a plus d'apparence qu'il y a autre chose que ce que *je vois* j'ai recherché si ce Dieu n'aurait point laissé quelque marque de soi. *Je vois* plusieurs religions contraires et partant toutes fausses, excepté une. [...]Chacun peut se dire prophète mais *je vois* la chrétienne et je trouve des prophètes, et c'est ce que chacun ne peut pas faire (num. 198).

The narrator grounds his argument in the very specific and forceful terms of looking and seeing. An initial and provocative visual experience — the sight of man's general blindness, moves his to widen the embrace of his looking and to gaze upon the universe around him. What he *sees* is silence:

[9] Pascal: *Pensées* in *Oeuvres complètes*, ed. Louis Lafuma (Paris: Seuil, 1963). Fragment num. 199. For the sake of simplicity, fragment numbers will henceforth be noted in the body of my text.

the mute universe offers no explanation, provides no relief to his anxiety. He turns then to those whom he sees around him. These others, having also looked around themselves and having, one may infer, seen the same blindness and mutism, opt to fix their gaze, to stop their search and give themselves over to the «quelques objets plaisants» that had by chance entered their field of vision.

For his part, the narrator does not yield to the attraction of these diversionary objects; but is moved by — and to — the thought that there is something more than what he sees immediately about him. This motivation directs him to look for any visible signs of God's presence, to raise his sights and extend his vision beyond the objects that impinge themselves too easily on his perception. What he sees is the Christian religion in which he finds prophets, that is, those able to see beyond and before the fact. In this, the Christian religion would strike him as fundamentally different from all those «religions contraires» that boldly claim themselves prophetical. The point may be short-sighted, even wrong; it is, nonetheless, wholly consonant with the methods and objectives of the apology. And part of the tactic of the apology is to induce the libertine audience to whom the text is supposedly directed to open its eyes, to take a look around, to use the physiological and psychological powers of sight and insight to arrive at an authentic perception and appreciation of the human condition.

In this perspective, he who fails to look directly at the evidence of man's misery will fail also to understand his grandeur. Moreover, the unauthentic looker/seeker is doomed to remain locked irretrievably in the prison-house of his own self-infatuation where he will have eyes only for himself. And his eyes will, in the end, have to fall on the same misery he would have refused to contemplate in the first place:

> [...] il veut être grand, *il se voit petit;* il veut être heureux, et *il se voit misérable;* il veut être parfait, et *il se voit plein d'imperfections;* il veut être l'objet de l'amour et de l'estime des hommes, et *il voit que ses défauts ne méritent que leur aversion et leur mépris.* Cet embarras où il se trouve produit en lui la plus injuste et la plus criminelle passion qu'il soit possible de s'imaginer [...] (num. 978).

Pascal makes a very definite stylistic choice here. There where he might have used more direct, but clearly less felicitous expressions such has «il est petit» and «il est plein d'imperfections», he uses «il se voit». It is, however, less to Pascail's point simply to state the obvious. Rather, he needs to have his reader sense himself looking at and recognizing himself in the mirror of the obvious. It is with a view towards this discovery process that the apologist has his first verb transmute into a an ironic phonological variant of itself: «voulouir» becomes «voir». Man's over-reaching and basic desire leads only to anti-climax and base disappointment. Dreams beget a dreary reality that weighs down on him («cet embarras où il se trouve»). The vision of his pettiness and defectiveness is the vision of his place in the order of things, hence the expression «il se voit» is made to melt into «il se trouve». Moreover, the weight of what he sees, «cet embarras», engenders in him «la plus injuste et plus criminelle passion qu'il soit possible d'imaginer». This untenable passion is nothing other than a secondary desire: the desire to hide from view his basic shortcomings and shortsightedness. Indeed, as if the very sight of his lack is the most wretched thing of all, «il met tout son soin à couvrir ses fautes et aux autres et à soi-même, et [...] il ne peut souffrir *qu'on les lui fasse voir ni qu'on les voie*». The desire for and movement towards illusion is fundamentally dangerous precisely because it is fundamentally blinding. And blindness, which here is self-inflicted, is a source of anguish. Indeed, it is not at all unlike the anguish felt by the person who, considering the «petite durée de [sa] vie absorbée dans l'éternité précédente et suivante», sees himself crushed in time and space, and is terrified and astonished to «see himself here rather than elsewhere». «*Je m'effraie et m'étonne de me voir ici plutôt que là*» (num. 68).

Not surprisingly, light and enlightenment are to be found in the religious tradition espoused by Pascal in his apology. On the eye-opening character of the Christian religion Pascal is most explicit: «Pour moi, j'avoue qu'aussitôt que la religion chrétiene découvre ce principe, que la nature de l'homme est corrompue et déchue de Dieu, *cela oeuvre des yeux à voir partout* le caractère de cette vérité.» (num. 471). To Pascal's eyes, to heed the call of Christianity is to accept the invitation, the challenge, of a clear view of man's greatness: «A mesure

143

qu'on a de lumière on découvre plus de grandeur et plus de grandeur et plus de bassesse dans l'homme. *Qui s'étonnera donc de voir* que la religion ne fait que connaître à fond ce qu'on reconnaît d'autant plus qu'on a plus de lumière (num. 613). The Christian religion would be the source of light and enlightenment. It would represent for Pascal an alternative to the most tragic kind of blindness associated with the human condition, namely, self-inflicted blindness. This is the blindness evoked in fragment 166: «Nous courons sans souci dans le précipice *après que nous avons mis quelque chose devant nous pour empêcher de le voir.*»

The attraction (and menace) of the precipice as well at the blind rush towards it are all of a piece in Pascal's argument. The oblivion of the abyss in the consequence, the desired consequence, of a willful refusal to see. And just as on the question of the void where Pascal had to convince a hesitant audience to look at the evidence of reality, in the *Apology* he sets to convince a similarly sceptical audience to take off its intellectual blinders and look intently into the void, into the emptiness of worldly diversion.

Louis A. MacKenzie
University of Notre Dame

THE ANTI-HERO JUAN DE AUSTRIA
IN *EL AGUILA DEL AGUA*

Luis Vélez de Guevara's historical play, *El águila del agua* (ca. 1640) [1], has not received much critical attention; unlike his other works, this *comedia* has seen only a scant line until the appearance of the 1986 edition [2]. The present study plans to remedy this previous neglect and show in detail various reflections on don Juan de Austria. Originally named Jeromín or Gerónimo, this future leader was born out of wedlock to the Emperor Charles V and Barbara Blomberg in Ratisbon in 1547 [3]. He was raised under the supervision of Luis Quesada in such secrecy that Philip II only learned of Juan's existence in 1558, after their father's death. Owing to his military genius, don Juan was given commands in the suppression of

[1] Michael G. Paulson and Tamara Alvarez-Detrell, *Lepanto: Fact, Fiction and Fantasy* (Lanham, MD: Univ. Press of America, 1986), contains the critical edition of this play and the data to determine its date of composition.

[2] The critics consulted for this paper include: Ramón Rozzell, ed., *La niña de Gómez Arias* (Granada: Univ. of Granada, 1959), 60-62; Edward Nagy, «El galeote de Lepanto de Luis Vélez de Guevara: la diversión en vez de escarmiento picaresco?», *Bulletin of the Comediantes,* 29, no. 1 (1977), 28-34; idem, «El galeote de Vélez de Guevara y el escarmiento alemanesco», *La Picaresca* (Actos del I Congreso internacional sobre la Picaresca), 833-834; Françoise Capdet et Jean Louis Flecniakoska, «Le Bâtard Don Juan d'Autriche, personnage de théâtre», *Dramaturge et Société,* ed. Jean Jacquot, 2 vols. (Paris: CNRS, 1968), I, 125-132; Theodor G. Ahrens, *Zur Charakteristik des Spanischen Dramas im Anfang des XVII. Jahrhunderts* (Halle: Waisenhauses, 1911).

[3] Cf. Paulson and Alvarez-Detrell, 32-34; Amarie Dennis, *Don Juan de Austria* (Madrid: Rivadeneyra, 1966); Jack Beeching, *The Galleys at Lepanto* (New York: Scribners, 1982), for information on don Juan's life and the battle of Lepanto.

the moriscos (1568) and at Lepanto (1571). Following the great naval battle, he found himself relegated to administrative posts in Italy and the Netherlands, where he died of fever in 1578. Philip II always respected his military genius, but never fully trusted him to act independently, and hence, kept don Juan from becoming too powerful.

El águila del agua concentrates on Juan in Spain and at Lepanto, where the play ends at the cessation of hostilities. This work is the dramatic sequel to Vélez's earlier *comedia*, *El hijo del águila*, which treats Juan de Austria's youth. In *El hijo*, the *águila* is the Emperor Carlos V, whom Frederick de Armas calls the «would-be universal ruler» [4], in whose shadow don Juan lives. Only the eagle could pass between the earth and the sun and look directly at the latter, according to mythological interpretation, which gives this imperial bird an inherent superiority over all others. In *El águila del agua*, Carlos V is long dead, although his name resurfaces periodically to haunt both Felipe II and don Juan. This chief eagle has left two eaglets to succeed him, but neither individually is as great as he. Felipe holds the throne and part of his empire, but lacks the military orientation of his father. Excluded from the Holy Roman Empire in 1555, the Prudent King has only the Spanish head of the bicephalous Habsburg eagle. Suffering from *soberbia*, Felipe gloats over his legitimate birth and his orderly succession to the throne, but fears competition from his younger sibling, don Juan. The latter possesses no legitimate claim to any throne, but can successfully lay claim to his father's martial capacity.

In *El águila del agua*, the eagle which Juan de Austria possesses is not a throne, but rather the eagle standards of the soldier. This *águila* assumes the form of the mythological Icarus (v. 3229) in his visions of flying near the sun. The sun and the throne attract him in his dream; as he «flies» too near both, the imperial sun of Felipe II melts his wings and precipitates him into the waters of Lepanto. Hence, Juan de Austria is *El águila del agua*, eagle for his father and his own military instincts, water for the only place he is completely successful and independent.

[4] Frederick A. de Armas, *The Return of Astraea: An Astral-Imperial Myth in Calderón* (Lexington: University of Kentucky Press, 1986), 124.

Venus plays a role in *El águila del agua* as a recurrent theme-image. In astrology, she is the sign which rules adolescence, and Juan's altercations with his nephew, don Carlos, show us that despite his chronological years, the naval hero acts and fights like an adolescent. Like a teenage boy, don Juan shows ambivalence toward members of the opposite sex; he knows instinctively that he should be drawn toward doña Hipólita, but he never feels secure or comfortable around her. Instead, he finds his security only in the company of male companions at sea.

Vélez makes a reference to Juan as Adonís, which refers back to Venus. Hipólita expresses her affection for the future naval hero, but this Adonis does not seem so interest in her. He appears more concerned with his own appearance, reputation and honor. Hipólita too takes on Venus' trappings following her wounding by the «dios ciego» (Cupid), and falls for Juan's physical charms, despite the fact that the latter does not return her affections. Our dramatist also refers to him as Narciso, the vain, spoiled, beautiful youth who fell in love with his own image. Juan does not show affection to earthly women, but remains faithful to the goddess Venus. The battle of Lepanto occurred as an immediate response to the Turkish menace to the isle of Cyprus. In Greco-Roman mythology, this island was sacred to Venus, and Vélez's unique reference (v. 2926) to the «isla de Venus» shows that he keeps the goddess in mind. If Juan's expedition was to rescue Venus (or at least her island), then the military youth was certainly in her service. If he failed to arrive in time, then he failed in his military duty to the goddess, just an he had failed her by not paying attention to Hipólita.

Three other mythological figures reoccur throughout the third act of the *comedia*: Marte, Neptuno and Jasón, all related to don Juan and the battle. Marte, god of war, appears in each act to prophecize our warrior's promise and effectiveness and to allow us to know that Lepanto is inevitable; this is, however, a bloodthisthy god, who cares little for the consequences of warfare. In this play, Juan de Austria shows concern only for his own honor and love of glory; his soldiers, rowers and companions can be easily sacrificed to bring him pleasure. When told that Escamilla has been impressed as a rower aboard the *Real* and when beseeched to grant him his freedom, don Juan disregards past friendship and thinks only of the opportunity to kill. Neptuno, god of the sea, reminds us that the Lepanto expedition is a sea enterprise, accomplished only with his cooperation and favorable Mediterranean conditions. Documented narratives of the battle reveal that despite signs of possibly incliment weather, the naval engagement took place under very favorable conditions. It is interesting to note that Juan de Austria's flagship, the *Real*, had representations of Neptuno in its decorations [5]. Jasón is known for his quest of the Golden Fleece and his courage on land and sea. Since Colchis, land of the Fleece, was under Ottoman control in 1571 and Juan promises to go there (vv. 1232-33), he is in effect the *nuevo Jasón*. The mythological Jasón had another side; he used his personal charms on Medea to assist him, but abandoned her once she was no longer useful. Hence, Juan like Jasón is an opportunist, quick to use people and then to cast them away when no longer necessary.

It seems no small coincidence that the deities mentioned in *El águila del agua* live on Mt. Olympus, in Turkish-dominated Greece. Juan de Austria, who has the characteristics and attributes of these gods, must try to liberate them; in a sense, the battle of Lepanto — which is represented on stage — defeats the oppressors of these multifaceted gods.

Vélez takes great liberties with persons and events. He has invented a personal rivalry between don Juan and don Carlos, which twice nearly brings the pair to blows. Historically, Juan de Austria was one of the few friends that Carlos had at court, but here Vélez uses don Carlos as a foil to provoke don Juan's insane jealousy and fiery temper. When the latter learns that his nephew has usurped his identity in order to seduce Hipólita, he flies into a rage, not so much for the attempted dishonor to the unfortunate woman as for the unauthorized use of his name and identity. Carlos serves to provoke his uncle in another way. While Juan is brave and militarily capable, Carlos shows sign of insanity and irrationality brought about through royal inbreeding; don Juan as a bastard can never legally hope to succeed to the Spanish throne, whereas the degenerate Carlos is the likely successor

---

[5] In the Reales Ataranzas in Barcelona is a full-sized reproduction of the *Real*, which follows the original. The Neptuno designs, as well as those dedicated to other deities, are readily visible.

to Felipe II. The reproach of illegitimacy and the riposte of merit taking precedence over «good birth» but no brains enlivens the first two acts of the play and the final act seems to demonstrate that Juan is correct; at Lepanto, Felipe and Carlos are no where to be seen and have been long since forgotten. Don Juan even boasts that he comes from a better father than don Carlos, a statement which disturbs even the usually calm don Felipe. Carlos seems to resent the fact that his uncle could have any woman he wants, but chooses not to, while he, the heir to the throne, chooses to have any woman, but cannot. Carlos and Felipe seem to resent the fact that they are but mere secretaries and courtiers, capable of waging war only in speech in writing, but are ignorant of actual practices. Historically, Carlos had nothing to do with the battle since he had been dead for nearly three years, and *el rey prudente* seemed relieved to have don Juan out of the country for a while. Felipe knew that while in battle, don Juan would not have time to seek a crown for himself.

Vélez researched the historical aspects of his subject matter throughly and saw no reason to juxtapose battle events as he had done in the case of the court scenes. Juan's participation in hand to hand combat, the presence of a female belligerent dressed like a male and the participation of a poet who resembled Cervantes give an air of accuracy ad authenticity to the third act. The Victor of Lepanto emerges as a brave warrior, even if he does seem somewhat of a braggart.

The *comedia* seems to reveal that within the central protagonist there is a complex character and that hence, two don Juan characters exist. The first is his real self, the young adolescent hedonist who seeks his own pleasure and the gratification of his libido. Juan loves only himself and uses every opportunity to admire himself: in the absence of mirrors in

---

6 In addition to the sources cited previously, I have also consulted the following accounts for battle information: Gianni Ballestreri, *Sebastiano Veneiro* (Rome: Ambrosini, 1971); Manuel Montero Hernando, *Juan de Austria* (n.p.: Silex, 1985); Robert Marx, *The Battle of Lepanto, 1571* (Cleveland: World Publishing, 1966); José María March, *La batalla de Lepanto* (Madrid: Ministerio de Asuntos Exteriores, 1944); Luciano Serrano, *España en Lepanto* (Madrid: Editorial Nacional, 1971); Halil Inacik, *The Ottoman Empire: The Classical Age, 1300-1600,* trans. Norman Itzkowitz and Colin Imber (New York: Praeger, 1973).

the play, the protagonist makes a fetish of his non-ocular reflections: his honor, glory and personal reputation. When entranced with himself, he ignores all others to gaze symbolically upon himself in a narcissist fashion. He likes other people only so long as they stimulate his ego and echo his praises. He is cruel and selfish and prone to fits of sado-masochism. He associates with characters such as don Carlos, who constantly reproach his illegitimacy and denigrate him in any way possible; following this verbal whipping, he turns on them and lashes them with epithets about their unsuitability and moral-physical flaws and attributes. These verbal abuses turn ugly as Juan reaches for his sword, which he intends to plunge into his adversaries as proof of his manhood as well as for personal gratification. Only the timely intervention of Felipe-Jupiter, as arbitrator of court and supreme being, prevents Juan and Carlos from dueling and sibling rivalry. It is interesting to note here that *El águilla del agua* is one of the few works on the don Carlos theme not to depict Felipe as a fanatical monster, but rather as a concerned father and peacekeeper. Don Juan and don Carlos certainly try his patience, but the king manages to maintain orden and prevent needless bloodshed. Felipe, although Juan's brother, is much older and here acts more like a father, much like the elder Tenorio in Tirso's play. He is disgusted with Juan's behavior and light attitude toward self-reform. Vélez makes several references to *El burlador de Sevilla* and its stone statue and *El águila* contains implications of «tan largo me lo fiáis». It seems no small coincidence that Vélez's protagonist has the same first name as Tirso's *burlador* and that both young men seem to derive their pleasure and gratification by hurting others rather than through coitus. Tirso's antagonist never learns to channel his energy to positive ends, but in the present play, Juan de Austria learns to turn his frustrations into service for God, king and country.

The second Juan de Austria remains hidden during the first two acts and reveals himself only in the third. Listening to Felipe's advice about not hurting others in Act Two, don Juan realizes that future confrontations with Carlos will cost him imprisonment and he enjoys brawling too much to reform completely. When the Pope's call for a crusade arrives, our protagonist quickly realizes his calling. Without self-reform, he can continue to kill, maim and injure others; if these «others» are Turks, Juan can be useful to the just cause of Christianity and be praised rather than censured for «brawling». Historically, we know that the fought bravely at Lepanto, was wounded several times and managed to carry the day through determined courage.

Prior to Lepanto, don Juan dreams of his glory in arms as he talks in his sleep. As he depicts his role in battle, he works himself up to a crescendo as an adolescent might during an erotic dream in which the culmination is the enemy fleeing before his unsheathed, moist sword, the sword often representing an erotic symbol. Given his propensity to expose his sword at the slightest pretext, we must not overlook the sexual significance of this act.

Don Juan incites his soldiers and sailors to fight the Turk and soon finds himself in the forefront of activity with his unsheathed sword striking right and left, killing with blessing of king and pope. The Turk begin with their insults of the young leader, who in turn works himself up to a frenzy with counter-insults and combat. At Lepanto, no one will prevent him from hurting others and deriving pleasure from it. He encourages his companions to strike, knowing fully well that some will fall in combat, but he cares little about the consequences. His *persona* as a great military leader causes all to praise him and he assumes this post with great personal pleasure. Vélez turns to speak praises of his military strategy, bravery and success, but the dramatist fully realizes that this *persona* merely covers Juan's baser nature. When Santa Cruz informs him of the total victory, Juan does not ask about Christian losses, but inquires only how much damage he has done. When the captured sons of the slain Alí Baja are ignominiously dragged before him, his only comment is «lloran». He shows them no compassion; their hurt is his pleasure, for their capture is another proof of his grandeur. At the close of the play, Juan de Austria is at the pinnacle of success. Lepanto is the highlight of his life as it is the *apogeo* of Spanish naval power. There is nothing greater to be hoped for, for him or for Spain. Lepanto is primarily his victory and only remotely the result of the other combattants' efforts.

The second don Juan is only superficially more noble than the first. Both operate from the same base instincts and

151

both derive pleasure from the sufferings of others. If the second *persona* seems a better man that the first, it is only because he has opportunistically seized the occasion of the national crisis and crusade to satisfy his lust for violence. The mythological images associated with don Juan give him greater-than-life-sized stature, but also seem to point at his larger-than-life-sized ego and base nature; he is an anti-hero rather than hero. The images highlight his shortcomings and seem to lead us to believe that at the cessation of hostilities at Lepanto, don Juan will revert to his original self. The *águila* which represents the noble standards of the empire also parallels Icarus' flight too close to the sun of glory and his subsequent fall. After Lepanto, his career takes him from arms and places him in administrative posts for which he is temperamentally unsuited. Lepanto is his sun and the cessation of hostilities will melt his wings and make him the *águila del agua,* the eagle from or in the water, sunk into oblivion after glorious flights toward grandeur. The play marks the protagonists progression through adolescence toward adulthood, but at the end of the *comedia,* don Juan de Austria remains an adolescent.

Michael G. Paulson
Kutztown University

EN BUSCA DEL HILO CONDUCTOR: ASEDIO AL INTERTEXTO Y A LA PERSONA POETICA EN *LINEA* DE GILBERTO OWEN

Al examinar el estilo complicado de *Línea* (1930), la colección de poemas en prosa del escritor mexicano contemporáneo Gilberto Owen (1904-1954), el lector se enfrenta con las oscuridades y con las porciones fragmentarias de pensamientos, que, como indica Merlin Forster, representan la inconexión de los sueños [1]. Por consiguiente, en *Línea* las oscuridades, contradicciones y desviaciones de la lógica requieren la participación activa del lector en la «naturalización» del texto. La poesía no es natural en el sentido de que nuestra atracción se basa en el hecho de que no constituye una comunicación habitual. Su cualidad formal y ficticia revela un vigor y una organización lingüística distinta al acto comunicativo común y corriente. Para experimentar ese vigor, el lector tiene que reducir la distancia entre su manera acostumbrada de comunicación y la «extraña» manera comunicativa del poema. Para lograr ese propósito tiene que leer el texto de acuerdo con los recursos propios del género poético. «La diferencia que es la fuente de valor se vuelve una distancia que debe franquearse a través de la actividad de lectura y de interpretación» [2].

Dejando a un lado por el momento los indicios que proporciona el aspecto intertextual, el cual se discutirá más adelante, es interesante notar cómo la misteriosa identidad del hablante en el poema «El hermano del hijo pródigo» sirve como recurso para iniciar al lector en la experiencia lírica.

---

[1] Merlin Forster, *Los Contemporáneos 1920-1932* (México: Ediciones de Andrea, 1964), p. 110.

[2] Jonathan Culler, *Structuralist Poetics* (Ithaca, New York: *Cornell University Press*, 1975), p. 134. La traducción de la cita es mía.

Ya el título del poema indica que su significado se desvía de la parábola tradicional. El hijo pródigo y no su hermano es generalmente el foco de atención. La siguiente alusión al hermano mayor en el poema es aún más enigmática: «y como ya todas se habrán casado, él, que es mi hermano mayor, no podrá aconsejarme la huida». En el texto bíblico el hermano mayor inequívocamente censura la huida del hijo pródigo. Aparte del hecho de que el título indica que el protagonista del poema vive a la sombra de otro más famoso, la relación con la parábola bíblica es ambigua; por consiguiente, es necesario buscar valor en otros elementos del poema y en la experiencia estética derivada del juego verbal del texto, y a través de estos elementos descubrir la relación entre la parábola y el poema.

EL HERMANO DEL HIJO PRODIGO

Todo está a punto de partir. Una cruz alada persigna al cielo. Los militares cortan las últimas estrellas para abotonarse el uniforme. Los árboles están ya formados, el menor tan lejano. Los corderos hacen el oleaje. Una casita enana se sube a una peña, para espiar sobre el hombro de sus hermanas, y se pone, roja, a llorar, agitando en la mano o en la chimenea su pañuelo de humo.

Detrás de los párpados está esperando este paisaje. ¿Le abriré? En la sala hay nubes o cortinas. A esta hora se encienden las luces, pero las mujeres no se han puesto de acuerdo sobre el tiempo, y el viajero va a extraviarse. —¿Por qué llegas tan tarde?, le dirán. Y como ya todas se habrán casado, él, que es mi hermano mayor, no podrá aconsejarme la huida.

Y en la oscuridad acariciaré su voz herida. Pero yo no asistiré al banquete de mañana, porque todo está a punto de partir y, arrojándose desde aquí, se llega ya muerto al cielo [3].

---

[3] Gilberto Owen, *Obras* (México: Letras Mexicanas, Fondo de Cultura Económica, 1979), p. 51. Todas las citas de esta obra se indicarán entre paréntesis en el texto.

Los ingeniosos juegos metafóricos del primer párrafo son una rica fuente de experiencias estéticas. «Una cruz alada persigna al cielo» es una metáfora que recuerda a López Velarde y su manera de describir una escena ordinaria en términos de la liturgia cristiana [4]. El acto habitual de abotonarse cobra magnitud e importancia porque los militares «cortan las últimas estrellas para abotonarse el uniforme». El efecto extraordinario se logra colocando un concepto dentro de una serie de conceptos que pertenecen a otra categoría. Al crear la ilusión de una fila de soldados, la formación de los árboles continúa el motivo familiar y añade al estatismo de los árboles la ilusión de movilidad. La economía verbal creada por las metáforas es sorprendente. Cuatro palabras, «el menor tan lejano», crean la impresión de una formación extensa de árboles que, como las otras imágenes, anuncian una ocasión solemne. La energía de las metáforas es sutil porque el efecto extraordinario o solemne se logra otorgando a un elemento ordinario —un ave, un botón, un árbol— una función superior. Los corderos que «hacen el oleaje» y la personificación de la casita enana «que se pone roja, a llorar, agitando en la mano o en la chimenea su pañuelo de humo» contribuyen a crear una escena de encantamiento y fábula.

Si el primer párrafo permite que el lector construya una explicación coherente de la escena se debe al hecho de que las comparaciones se basan en semejanzas objetivas (el ave se parece a una cruz o un rebaño de corderos se parece a la espuma de las olas, etc.), y de ese modo permite formular una idea del tema. Al personificar los objetos y elaborarlos metafóricamente, el narrador elude una descripción sentimental y capta el momento de anticipación y energía de una partida, así como el impacto emotivo que resulta cuando se deja atrás lo acostumbrado para emprender nuevos caminos y nuevas aventuras.

El segundo párrafo y el último no exhiben la misma regularidad del primero y consisten en una serie de preguntas y declaraciones, en apariencia inconexas, y en la falta de una

---

[4] En «Mi corazón se amerita...», López Velarde describe el amanecer y la puesta del sol de la siguiente manera: «la estola violeta en los hombros del alba, / el cíngulo morado de los atardeceres, / los astros, y el perímetro jovial de las mujeres», en López Velarde, *Obras*, ed. de José Luis Martínez (México, FCE, 1971), pp. 154-155.

persona poética definible. Las oscuridades y los fragmentos de pensamientos impiden una formulación coherente de la escena. El efecto es de titubeo e incertidumbre como si el narrador estuviera soñando o ebrio. La yuxtaposición de párrafos tan disímiles resulta en la búsqueda de orden y continuidad en los párrafos fragmentados y la revaluación del primer párrafo a la luz de los dos últimos [5].

No queda claro cuál es la conexión entre el narrador en primera persona de los dos últimos párrafos y el viajero al que éste alude o la escena descrita en el primer párrafo. La imposibilidad de construir al sujeto de la partida se debe tal vez al hecho de que éste no exista, de que el viaje sea solamente la proyección del sueño o del deseo del narrador. La primera frase del segundo párrafo: «detrás de los párpados está esperando este paisaje» sugiere un sueño. El poema presenta a un hijo pródigo que sueña la partida, pero que es incapaz de emprenderla; es decir, una imagen invertida de su hermano bíblico y, por consiguiente, subraya la tensión entre la aventura simbolizada por el hijo pródigo tradicional y su propia inmovilidad. Nótese que la movilidad o partida sólo se da en términos de objetos estáticos (la casa, los árboles) y de los animales (el ave y los corderos), a los que se alude solamente en tercera persona. El «yo» no participa de la escena y al describirla en tercera persona revela su posición marginada en relación a un centro de actividad vital. En contraste con la claridad, el ambiente de fábula y el espíritu de anticipación de la descripción, el resto del poema revela sentimientos de incertidumbre, titubeo y desilusión: la falta de acuerdo entre las mujeres, la preocupación de que el viajero se extravíe y pierda la oportunidad de tener éxito contribuyen a la sensa-

---

[5] La súbita ruptura de la continuidad narrativa dentro de un mismo poema se prefigura en un poema de López Velarde, «El retorno maléfico», estudiado por Eugene Moretta. La discontinuidad se manifiesta, observa Moretta, entre las seis primeras estrofas en las que un «hijo pródigo» se imagina de regreso a su hogar destrozado y la última estrofa en la cual predominan oraciones incompletas, expresiones redundantes y la desaparición del yo poético. La fragmentación verbal refleja la propia desolación del protagonista y acusa la técnica de la enumeración caótica que tendrá su auge en el surrealismo. En «López Velarde y Owen. Examen de una influencia», *Gilberto Owen en la poesía mexicana* (México: Fondo de Cultura Económica, 1985), páginas 52-54.

ción de vacilación. La ambigüedad se extiende al nivel gramatical. Cuando el narrador pregunta: ¿Le abriré?, no queda claro si se refiere al paisaje, que en este caso está invertido porque está detrás de los párpados.

Al unirse dos perspectivas disímiles —una de encantamiento y esperanza y la otra repleta de incertidumbre y de temor— la problemática que se explora es la manera de crear un puente entre el ensueño y la pesadilla. Esta problemática es significativa: la falta de coherencia y la presencia de personas mixtas (no queda claro si las varias personas que aparecen en el poema son distintas manifestaciones de una misma persona) suspenden el poema en el limbo de la indeterminación y de la inmovilidad. Hay varias alusiones a circunstancias que posiblemente impidan la acción en el momento propicio: si las luces no se encienden a tiempo, si se llega demasiado tarde, si es imposible aconsejar la huida [6]. «El hermano del hijo pródigo» prefigura en forma esquemática uno de los poemas de mayor alcance lírico de Owen, «Sindbad el varado». En este poema elabora el tema del estancamiento verbal y existencial mediante la figura legendaria de Sindbad, el marino de *Las mil y una noches*. Como en «El hermano del hijo pródigo», logra establecer una insólita tensión lírica entre la fábula y el vacío existencial. La imagen del «yo» exiliado de toda fuente vital está casi siempre presente en la obra de Owen, lo cual «comprueba la observación de Octa-

---

[6] Como Hamlet, el narrador lucha con los fantasmas de una pesadilla, pero es incapaz de tomar una acción (emprender la partida) o aprovecharse del momento oportuno que le permita realizar el ideal deseado. «El hermano del hijo pródigo» recuerda también a los hombres huecos rellenos de paja de T. S. Eliot que sufren las torturas de no tomar ningún curso de acción. Son sombras incapaces de salir en pos del cuerpo, destinados al vacío y a mantenerse anónimos aun ante sí mismos: «Cuerpo sin forma, matiz sin color, fuerza paralizada, acción sin movimiento», «The Hollow Men», primera estrofa, versos 12-13 (traducción mía). La parálisis de la voluntad es un tema elaborado a lo largo de la obra de Owen. En relación con el poema del día seis, «El hipócrita» de «Sindbad el varado», García Terrés señala la ironía del protagonista que quisiera hacer pasar su fatiga y sus actos pecaminosos por la virtuosa «muerte de todos los sentidos» que preconizan los místicos. En García Terrés, *Poesía y alquimia. Los tres mundos de Gilberto Owen* (México: Ediciones Era, 1980), p. 116.

vio Paz de que en la poesía de Owen "el tema del naufragio y el de la inmovilidad no son dos, sino uno y el mismo"»[7].

En el poema que estamos analizando la voz herida sugiere la parálisis verbal que experimenta el hermano del hijo pródigo al naufragar en la pesadilla de la esterilidad. El cielo al que se llega ya muerto es el paraíso anhelado e inalcanzable. Según la parábola bíblica, el hijo pródigo se extravía porque actúa impulsivamente y regresa a su pueblo arrepentido. El símbolo de su redención es el banquete en el hogar paterno. Aunque el poema de Owen da lugar a meditaciones morales relacionadas con el problema de la esterilidad que resulta de la inacción, una explicación ética del asunto es insuficiente. La laguna entre el ensueño de la partida y la pesadilla de la impotencia es difícil de franquear porque la meditación sobre el curso de acción revela la naturaleza esquiva de la trayectoria y del consiguiente galardón anhelado o «banquete de mañana». La laguna, que es la fuente de valor en el poema, también es fuente de indeterminación y perplejidad ante la fugacidad de cualquier significado estable y satisfactorio.

Aunque la conclusión a que ha llevado la lectura de «El hermano del hijo pródigo» ilumina la estructura y los posibles significados del poema, es interesante observar cómo el poema «dificulta la construcción de una persona poética» y «depende para sus efectos del hecho de que el lector tratará de construir una posición enunciativa»[8].

«Le Retour de L'enfant prodigue» de André Gide proporciona otra perspectiva al poema de Owen. Gide reelabora la parábola bíblica y añade a su versión a un hermano menor, quien encarna el ideal de libertad individual frente a la rigidez de los valores consagrados por las instituciones sociales. En la versión de Gide, el hijo pródigo regresa porque se lleva consigo la herencia del hogar paterno. Al enfrentarse con los peligros de la trayectoria, vuelve, porque prefiere refugiarse en la seguridad de un orden establecido, aunque ese refugio represente la uniformidad por sobre la espontaneidad que su

---

[7] Eugene Moretta, p. 40. La cita de Paz proviene de *Sombras de obras* (Barcelona: Seix Barral, 1983), p. 289. Quiero manifestar mi deuda para con Moretta en cuanto a las ideas relacionadas con el tema del exilio en «Sindbad el varado».

[8] Culler, p. 170.

viaje prometía. La misión redentora de forjar una persona-
lidad individual abierta a aires renovadores y libre de las
estrecheces reconfortantes —aunque dicha libertad lleve a la
desesperación— recae sobre el hermano menor. El saldrá sin
la herencia paterna, puesto que el camino ha sido preparado
por su hermano mayor [9].

Es evidente que Owen basó su poema en la obra de Gide;
sin embargo, como el protagonista de Owen es un viajero
inmóvil en la pesadilla de la esterilidad, su persona contrasta
irónicamente con el ideal gideano de libertad, espontaneidad
y realización personal. Lo que separa al protagonista de Owen
de una trayectoria vital no tiene una definición clara y se expresa mediante un personaje que está ausente del escenario
donde se llevan a cabo las batallas heroicas (las partidas) y las
antiheroicas (los regresos fallidos). El protagonista sueña la
escena de la partida, pero es incapaz de integrarse a ella, por
lo cual prosigue a la descripción de lo que le es más inme-
diato: la duda, la vacilación y la esterilidad. El valor del
poema reside en retratar el anhelo del ser humano de parti-
cipar en un escenario donde pueda desempeñar un papel
significativo y vital y su angustia frente a los obstáculos que
le impiden el acceso a esa realidad.

SOMBRA

Mi estrella —óyela correr— se apagó hace años.
Nadie sabría ya de dónde llega su luz, entre los dedos
de la distancia. Te he hablado ya, Nathanael, de los cuerpos sin sombra. Mira ahora, mi sombra sin cuerpo. Y el
eco de una voz que no suena. Y el agua de ese río que,
arriba, está ya seco, como al cerrarle de pronto la llave
al surtidor, el chorro mutilado sube un instante todavía.
Como este libro entre tus manos, Nathanael.

(*Obras,* pág. 51.)

---

[9] Esta interpretación está basada en el estudio de Kenneth Perry,
«Petite Oeuvre de Circonstance», *The Religious Symbolism of André
Gide* (The Hague: Mouton & Co., 1969).

Aunque los poemas de *Línea* se caracterizan por su estructura fragmentaria, el título sugiere un orden ininterrumpido y continuo, la posibilidad de hallar en el laberinto lingüístico un hilo conductor o un sistema que permita experimentar las dimensiones poéticas del lenguaje sin extraviarse por senderos estériles. Uno de los hilos conectivos que se hace perceptible entre la fragmentación verbal de «Sombra» es la relación del poema con otros textos. El enigmático Nathanael al que se dirige el narrador es un personaje derivado de *Los alimentos terrestres* de André Gide. Dice Owen en su selección en prosa titulada «André Gide» que fue durante la lectura de los *Morceaux choisis*

> cuando ocurrió mi primer encuentro con Menalcas y cuando inicié, por mi cuenta, un diálogo imposible con un Nathanael, nacido sordo y mudo por la propia voluntad de monólogos sin respuesta del padre, quien además debería de preferir que no le oyera para que le olvidara con más premura. O eso al menos era lo que entonces me complacía yo en entender, todavía insospechables para mí la desnudez o la sinceridad de Gide.

(*Obras*, pág. 247.)

Lo que aparenta ser un simple diálogo entre dos personajes líricos es, en efecto, un diálogo intertextual. El enigmático Nathanael, con un libro apropiadamente entre las manos, su giere no sólo su propia función literaria, sino la del narrador, cuyo poema absorbe y transforma el texto de Gide y la del lector que consiste en leer el poema en relación con otros textos.

Para experimentar las amplias dimensiones de «Sombra» es necesario, por consiguiente, releer el poema a la luz de los textos con los que está relacionado explícita e implícitamente. Este proceso de enriquecimiento, revitalización o renovación requiere la continua actividad textual. Tal es el descubrimiento que hace Owen en la frase de Gide: «sólo escribo para ser releído» (*Obras*, pág. 247). El poema es un vehículo hacia una visión más amplia, y en ese sentido constituye una fuerza liberadora. Sin embargo, la selección en prosa de Owen alude a su propio «cautiverio lírico» y al de Nathanael. «Sombra» insistentemente llama la atención hacia imágenes mutiladas y estériles: a una estrella apagada, a los cuerpos sin sombra, a una voz que no suena y al libro de Nathanael que se compara a un chorro mutilado y a un río seco. La duplicidad que se observa en los tres textos no permite una interpretación unívoca y revela la naturaleza equívoca de la actividad literaria, ya un cautiverio, ya una libertad [10]. Las imágenes estériles subrayan la dificultad del proceso lírico que requiere el distanciamiento de los límites confortantes y acostumbrados, y engendra la angustia, el temor y la frustración de extraviarse en un silopsismo hermético donde el sutil eslabón entre el discurso literario y el habitual se vuelve imperceptible o parece desaparecer por completo. El abandonarse, como observa Owen, «a la peligrosa y terrible penitencia de perderme en ese infierno que va rodando en pos de Dios por todas las pasiones» (*Obras*, pág. 248).

El ideal esquivo se expresa mediante expresiones particularmente brillantes y sonoras en «Sombra»: «*Mi estrella*—óyela correr—se apagó hace años. Nadie sabría de dónde llega su luz, entre los dedos de la distancia». La sensación de pérdida y alienación se manifiesta en la separación de elementos cuya división es imposible en un contexto real: «Te he hablado ya, Nathanael, de los cuerpos sin sombra. Mira ahora mi sombra sin cuerpo».

De la misma manera que los textos de Gide proporcionan una nueva perspectiva sobre la esterilidad de Nathanael para Owen, las imágenes estériles de «Sombra» requieren una relectura en relación con el texto en prosa de Owen. La relectura es vital. La afirmación de Gide lleva a Owen a descubrir la sutil ironía a que está sujeto Nathanael: «que el insistente grito que ordena a Nathanael emanciparse del lírico cautiverio quiere decir precisamente lo contrario: No arrojes este libro y no partas — y no asumas verdadera una libertad que nunca he deseado ofrecerte» (*Obras*, pág. 247).

[10] Frederick Jameson, *The Prison House of Language* (Princeton, N. J.: Princeton University Press, 1972). El signo, observa Jameson, es de algún modo impuro. Nuestra incertidumbre ante él, su ambigüedad (ya una transparencia, ya un obstáculo, puro sonido y puro significado) resulta no tanto de nuestro conocimiento imperfecto del fenómeno, sino que está fundada más bien en la estructura misma del lenguaje (traducción mía), p. 173.

Aunque la experiencia del ideal esquivo y de la esterilidad son partes integrantes del proceso literario, es posible hallar valor en la interacción de un texto con el otro. Owen admite que su teoría cronológica es un tanto «traída de los cabellos» porque cuando quiere descubrir algo nuevo en *Los alimentos,* prefiere leerlo en *El inmoralista,* una obra publicada cinco años más tarde, pero que según Owen debió de escribirse simultáneamente. En *El inmoralista* descubre «el diario que explica en Michael lo que Gide vivía y pensaba y sufría al escribirlos» (*Obras,* pág. 248). Aunque sería traído de los cabellos sugerir que el texto en prosa de Owen, publicado por lo menos quince años después de *Línea,* se escribiera simultáneamente, no hay duda de que la lectura de «Sombra» en relación al texto de Owen y al de Gide proporciona un hilo conductor que realza nuestra experiencia lírica.

Georgina J. Whittingham
State University of New York

INDICE